Partnerships to Improve Access and Quality of Public Transport

Partnerships to Improve Access and Quality of Public Transport

A Case Report: Colombo, Sri Lanka

SEVANATHA Urban Resources Centre

Edited by M. Sohail

Water, Engineering and Development Centre
Loughborough University
2003

Water, Engineering and Development Centre,
Loughborough University,
Leicestershire, LE11 3TU, UK

© WEDC, Loughborough University, 2003

ISBN 13 Paperback: 978 1 84380 036 1
ISBN Ebook: 9781788533188
Book DOI: http://dx.doi.org/10.3362/9781788533188

A catalogue record for this book is available from the British Library.

A reference copy of this publication is also available online at:
http://www.lboro.ac.uk/wedc/publications/

SEVANATHA Urban Resources Centre (2003)
Partnerships to Improve Access and Quality of Public Transport - A Case Report: Colombo, Sri Lanka
Series Editor: M. Sohail

WEDC (The Water, Engineering and Development Centre) at Loughborough University in the UK is one of the world's leading institutions concerned with education, training, research and consultancy for the planning, provision and management of physical infrastructure for development in low- and middleincome countries.

This edition is reprinted and distributed by Practical Action Publishing.
Since 1974, Practical Action Publishing has published and disseminated books and information in support of international development work throughout the world. Practical Action Publishing trades only in support of its parent charity objectives and any profits are covenanted back to Practical Action (Charity Reg. No. 247257, Group VAT Registration No. 880 9924 76).

This document is an output from a project funded by the UK
Department for International Development (DFID)
for the benefit of low-income countries.
The views expressed are not necessarily those of DFID.

Designed at WEDC by Glenda McMahon, Sue Plummer and Rod Shaw

Acknowledgements

The Sevanatha Research Team would like to extend their sincere gratitude to the following persons, who have assisted the project activities in numerous ways. Without their support and contributions it would not have been possible to produce this research report. They include:

- Dr. M. Sohail Khan, Research Manager, Institute of Development Engineering, WEDC, Civil and Building Engineering Department, Loughborough University, UK

- The members of the Research Advisory Committee

- The President of the Private Bus Owners Association of Sri Lanka

- The Secretary General of the Passenger Association of Sri Lanka

- The community leaders of the six urban poor settlements where case studies were carried out

- The members of the households of the six urban poor settlements who provided information for the research study

- The officials of the government institutions and local authorities concerned

- The staff of Sevanatha organization, including the President of Sevanatha, Programme Managers, Field Staff and the Office Secretary

H.M.U. Chularathna
Coordinator
SEVANATHA Research Team

List of boxes

List of tables

Contents

vii

Section 1

Introduction

1.1 Project details

This report presents the findings of the Research Project R 7866, *Partnerships to improve access and quality of urban public transport for the urban poor*, carried out by a research team of the Sevanatha Urban Resource Centre, Colombo in collaboration with the Water, Engineering and Development Centre (WEDC) of the Loughborough University in the United Kingdom. The project was sponsored by the Department for International Development (DFID) of the British Government.

1.2 Background to the project

Poverty is the key factor that affects development worldwide, especially in the lesser-developed countries. A host of factors in social, economic and political spheres have led these countries' poor situations. Poverty is a vicious circle, which traps and pushes people towards ever poorer conditions. For instance, unstable economic conditions impair a country's ability to provide better services for its people, and lack of access to good services leads that situation further downwards. In transport, if people are getting a substandard service, not only will it affect their livelihoods, but also the service itself will not be sustainable as a profitable venture, leading to its own downturn. Efforts to alleviate poverty should thus understand and address both the causes and effects of poverty simultaneously. This should entail actions in the widest social, economic and political spectrums.

Alleviation of poverty is among the highest political goals of all developing nations and, at the same time, the key objective of any international development policy forum. In implementing projects that are focused on the alleviation of poverty, international donors play a vital role, helping developing nations with financial and technical assistance. The Department for International Development (DFID) in the United Kingdom is one such donor, with its key strategies encompassing:

- policies and actions, which promote sustainable livelihoods;

- better education, health and opportunities for the empowerment of poor people; and

- protection and better management of the natural and physical environment.

In the process of making actions happen at ground level, DFID relies on a holistic approach, identifying the key policies and practices that will improve the livelihoods of the poor. 'Sustainable Livelihoods' (SL) is one such approach, which takes into account the multi-faceted nature of any particular issue to be addressed. This study summarizes

1

the findings resulting from the application of this approach to the issue of urban public transport.

Box 1.1. Definition of slums

Preparation of the Policy Paper on Slum and Shanty Upgrading in Colombo Municipal Council area by the Slum and Shanty Division of the Urban Development Authority of the Ministry of Local Government, Housing and Construction in 1979 was the first ever attempt taken by the government to identify slum and shanties (low-income settlements) for a larger development programme in the city of Colombo. The policy paper was the first official document that had categorized slums into different categories and identified them for development purposes. According to the above document, slums are defined as follows.

'Slums are old tenements created to accommodate the influx of a new labour force into the city during a period when the thriving plantation industry required labour for processing, packaging, storing, handling and shipping activities. Tenement units normally consist of a single bedroom, a small veranda and a living area with common water taps and latrine facilities. They were usually built in rows on a block of land commonly referred to as a garden. These so-called tenements contain anything between a group of two or three units, and a few hundreds arranged in rows.'

Old residential buildings (slum houses) in former residential areas, mainly in older parts of Colombo north and central (e.g. Petta, Hultsdrop, Wolfendhal), later became apartments for low-income workers. They were subdivided into small units, inadequately maintained and largely deprived of basic sanitary facilities. In local language these types of settlement arrangements are called 'Mudukku'. People who live in these types of houses do not like calling their houses by official names. They themselves identify them as 'Row Houses'-'Peli Geval'.

Box 1.2. Shanties (squatter settlements)

The shanties are a collection of small single units of improvised structures, constructed with non-durable materials on vacant land throughout the city. Shanties illegally occupy state or private land usually with no regular water, sanitation or electricity supply. The majority of them are built on land that is subject to frequent flooding.

In local language these types of settlements are called 'Pelpath'. This term reflects a group of people who are living in more difficult conditions and greater poverty than Mudukku or slum settlements.

1.2.1 The urban context

The rate of urbanization, especially in the developing countries, is phenomenal today posing serious challenges to the governments of the respective countries in providing essential urban services for their ever-increasing urban populations. Higher competition often sidelines the urban poor, shrinking their ability to access such services, and pushing them towards more vulnerable situations. What is also noteworthy is that in most developing countries, the poor consist of a substantial percentage of the country's urban population, which in some cases even goes beyond the halfway mark.

Box 1.3. Low-cost flats, relocated housing and old deteriorated quarters

For the above categories of low-income houses, there was no official definition found. However, the officials of urban local authorities and other relevant departments, as well as the local politicians understand them as follows.

Low-cost flats

Low-cost flats are those walk-up apartments (ground + one or two floors maximum) built by the agencies such as Colombo Municipal Council, the Department of Railways etc., for their workers who are mostly the blue-collar workers. These were built during the 1960s and 1970s and were provided with shared toilet and water facilities.

The low-cost flats consist of housing units mostly with two bedrooms, a kitchen and a small veranda allocated to an employee and his/her family for rent. The agreement seems to be that when the particular employee retires from his/her job, he has to return the housing unit to the authority. However, in practice what happened was that when the original employee retired he used to find employment in the same organization for his son or daughter and thus requested that the authority retain for the house for the family. In this way, these low-cost flats have become inherited houses for one or two generations. Usually, the quality of the flats is very poor due to lack of maintenance. On the other hand, the occupants pay only a marginal rent, which is not sufficient to make any significant improvement. Thus, they have become neglected low-cost flats.

Relocated housing

Relocated housing are those low-income settlements affected as a result of canal improvement, road improvement or other development activities carried out mainly by the government whose residents were subsequently relocated to another location or locations. Most of the relocated housing areas in Colombo were provided with common amenities, an individual housing lot and a housing loan for constructing a basic house. Subsequently, over the years, the communities organize themselves to active community groups and through local politicians they request individual amenities. After about five to 10 years they became developed low-income settlements.

Old deteriorated quarters

The old deteriorated quarters are to those single storey row houses occupied mainly by the minor employees (sanitary workers etc.) of the municipality. These houses belong to the Municipal Council. They were built over 30–40 years ago and were not maintained properly, hence are neglected. These houses are located mostly within the inner-city areas and have become congested as the families began to grow and occupy in the same housing unit.

In an urban context transport is a key service, which directly influences the livelihood pattern of any social stratum. Those with higher levels of income have more transport options as they can afford private modes, whereas people of lower income levels mostly resort to public transport.

This study examines the accessibility issues relating to public transport by the urban poor in accessing to their daily activities, which invariably affects their income and livelihood pattern.

In this context, the main emphasis of the study was to investigate the methods of providing urban public transport, its quality and accessibility to the poor. The focus area of the study was city of Colombo, the capital city of Sri Lanka.

1.2.2 Sustainable livelihoods approach

Poverty is now recognized as a condition that goes beyond mere lack of basic income. It is considered to have multi-dimensional characteristics and causes. For instance, in Colombo, Sri Lanka, the slum and shanty settlements (squatters) are now considered as 'underserved' and not solely as a concentration of 'low-income' communities. Residents of such settlements engage mainly in the informal economic activities of the city to earn their living. In terms of income, they are on a par with some of the formal sector employment categories such as peons, clerks, skilled labour etc. or may even be earning more. However, the people living in these underserved settlements are not regarded equals in the mainstream social organization, particularly due to the social stigma attached to their being members of deprived communities—a prevalent social division in Colombo.

Colombo's underserviced settlements have been identified as slums, shanties, upgraded and relocated settlements by different development programmes implemented in the past. Of these, the slum and squatter settlements are concentrated in close proximity to the town centre. Squatters usually occupy reservation lands, canal banks or private lands, which are subdivided into small plots over a long period of time along with extended families. Most of these settlements do not have land ownership. Their plot sizes range from $20m^2$ to $50m^2$. Some of these settlements were 'upgraded' under the government housing programmes launched in the early 1980s, namely the Hundred Thousand Houses Programme and the million houses programme. Under the same housing programmes those settlements, which had already been located on lands suitable for habitation, were upgraded *in-situ* by providing basic infrastructure and housing loans, thereby encouraging the dwellers to build their houses using permanent building materials. The relocated settlements are the ones that have been shifted from their original lands due to various reasons, such as road and canal expansions, flooding and land acquisition by the government for various development purposes. Even on the relocated settlements the maximum plot area a family gets is $50m^2$. The legal plot size of a residential plot is $300m^2$ in the city as per the prevalent building regulations. However, the government took a decision in the early 1980s to relax the above plot size requirement to $50m^2$ for upgrading the low-income settlements, identifying such areas as special project areas. This can be regarded as a progressive step taken by the government of Sri Lanka in its efforts to solve the housing problem of the urban poor. The relocated settlements were mostly located a few kilometres away from town centres. At the time of relocation (by a government authority) each family was given a $50m^2$ lot of land. Basic settlement layout plans were prepared in consultation with the families concerned by the officials of the National Housing Development Authority (NHDA), providing the access roads and some basic facilities, such as common water taps and common toilets.

Thus these settlements, with or without planned interventions, are still called underserved today, as they do not get the desired service standards in terms of the provision of water, electricity, sewage, and garbage disposal. The settlements, including those that were subjected to planned interventions, fall under the category of 'special projects' by the Urban Development Authority (UDA). The major reason that lies behind this categorization is attached to the relaxation of legal plot size, set back requirements and the width of road frontage etc. Accordingly, the reduced plot size is between $20m^2$ to $50m^2$, whereas it is $300m^2$ as per the normal building regulations in the city.

A majority of the inhabitants of these settlements are unskilled labourers and minor employees of public and private sector organizations. As cited earlier, they resort to a variety of informal income-generating activities. These include pavement hawking, working at wholesale vegetable markets, running small businesses in the neighbourhoods, such as boutiques, mobile vending, working as housemaids, fish and vegetable vending, collecting recyclable materials, repair of household items etc. Some of them even resort to selling and trafficking drugs, selling illicit liquor and other socially unacceptable businesses.

The cumulative effects of the causes and the manifestation of poverty are clearer within the context 'underserved', which has eventually pushed these people towards major social 'segregation'. They lack social identity and recognition, as neither these settlements nor the inhabitants are considered 'respectable' or 'equals' among mainstream civil society. Locally they are called '*Mudukku*' or '*Watta*' people, which means people from slum communities in the city.

Thus, the plight of the underserved settlements is manifold. First and foremost they do not get the standard of services that exists in other residential areas of the city. Even if the inhabitants make a claim for land ownership, the land would still be much below the standard legal plot size of a residential house in the city. This factor makes these settlements fall under 'special regulations' within the regulatory mechanisms, and they thus do not gain the same status of other residential neighbourhoods. Therefore, the inhabitants of the underserved settlements are not considered eligible to pay rates to the Municipal Council. Consequently, the settlers inherit a lower social ranking, both as a group and as individuals, and the pressure of this social stigma makes it extremely difficult for them to rise above their situation. However, since about the mid-1990s, the Municipal Council of Colombo has been seriously discussing the issue of integrating the upgraded urban poor settlements into the mainstream housing in the city. As a first step towards this aim, the Council has taken the initiative of collecting property rates from selected upgraded low-income settlements on a flat rate basis for all individual housing units. In certain upgraded low-income settlements, property rates are being charged on individual property value basis. Therefore, it may be considered that such progressive moves could pave the way in the future for gradual integration of the urban poor into the mainstream of city life and procedures.

The appropriateness of the Sustainable Livelihoods (SL) approach is felt within this context to strengthen the life of the urban underserved settlers, both quantitatively and qualitatively. It is a holistic approach and in application it begins by a careful analysis of what a livelihood has already got as assets—both material and social—of a particular group of households or a community. A livelihood becomes sustainable when it can withstand and recover from stresses and shocks and maintain and improve its capabilities and assets both now and in the future (DFID, 1999).

Ashley and Carney (1999:6–7) provide a working definition of sustainable livelihoods and core principles of the SL approach, which have been adapted for this study.

Sustainable livelihoods
A sustainable livelihood is a way of thinking about the objectives, scope and priorities for development, in order to enhance progress in poverty elimination. A livelihood comprises capabilities, assets and activities required for the act of living.

Core principles of SL

People-centred. It is of primary importance to be people-centred if poverty elimination is to be meaningful. Thus, this research focuses on urban underserved communities and on issues relating to transport that influence their livelihoods.

Responsive and participatory. The research takes the key actors as its research base, including the people themselves who use public transport, service providers and regulatory personnel. It takes into account **user perceptions** on issues relating to urban transport.

Multi-level. Elimination of the causes and effects of poverty requires exploring macro and micro factors that influence the livelihoods of the urban poor. Thus the research explores issues relating to both the micro and macro levels of policy and operational aspects of public transport. The link between policy and practice is one of the key concerns of the research, which concerns both the historical perspective and the present context.

Conducted in partnership. Partnerships in public transport are in operation both in the public and private sectors, formally and informally (para-transport). Bus transport is operated by both these sectors, while rail transport is under the monopoly of the government. Also para-transport modes such as three-wheelers, private school and office vans are in operation.

Thus perspectives from all the key actors under these partnerships are taken into account.

Sustainable. The four key dimensions of sustainability: economic, institutional, social and environmental, are envisaged in the study. Evolution of transport policies, their operational aspects and the present context in terms of sustainable development, are studied.

Dynamic. Key milestones in the socio-economic and political spheres that have taken place in the past and up to the present have a direct impact on the livelihoods of the urban poor and on the provision of urban transport. These were explored in the study to understand what mechanisms might contribute to improving the access to and quality of urban transport, through partnerships.

1.3   The study context

Public transport has been a hot issue in social economic and political settings, particularly since the mid-20th century in Sri Lanka, although it does not seem to have been taken as a part of the comprehensive vision of a sustainable livelihood approach. It is also notable that less emphasis has been paid to user perceptions, with a view to influencing and guiding the policies of public transport. Most studies carried out in the past have shown rather segmented approaches and have thus failed to visualize transport as an integral part of the development process of a given physical setting. The inseparable link between public transport and people's livelihoods, especially of the lower income categories, needs to be envisaged at depth. Any policy forum should essentially take transport users' views and suggestions into account if transport policies are to be led to viable solutions.

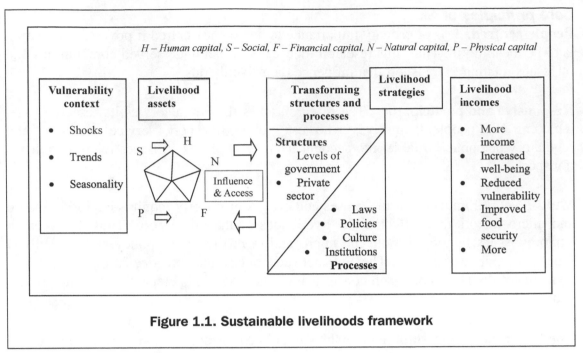

Figure 1.1. Sustainable livelihoods framework

Source: Ashley and Carney, 1999

Urban contexts pose unique challenges in urban transport due to their extreme population concentrations, focused economic activities, high susceptibility to change, social, economic and cultural diversity and associated issues. Colombo is the largest city in Sri Lanka, with a residential population of about 0.64 million and a daily commuter population of about 400,000.

Despite various measures, public transport continues with the same prolonged issues, both in Sri Lanka and in Colombo. Within the City of Colombo, still nearly 50 per cent of the population lives in poor urban settlements. They are the most vulnerable social category, affected by inadequate urban services, including lack of proper public transport services. As per a recent study, it has been found that there are 1,614 urban poor settlements scattered in and around the City of Colombo (Poverty Profile, City of Colombo, February 2002).

In terms of the number of families, these urban poor settlements accommodate about 77,612 families. The Colombo Municipal Council area has been divided into 47 municipal wards and these 47 wards are grouped into six municipal districts for administrative purposes. The survey carried out for the Poverty Profile for Colombo City in 2002 revealed that urban poor settlements are located in almost all the 47 municipal wards, ranging from four settlements to 73 in a ward (see Annex 1).

The distribution of urban poor settlements by municipal districts is shown below.

As per the above data, it is evident that Districts 1, 2A and 2B, which belong to the Colombo Central and North areas, comprise about 73 per cent of all the urban poor settlements of the city. The Municipal Districts 3, 4 and 5, which are located towards Colombo East and the southern direction, contain fewer (27 per cent) of the city's urban settlements. The primary reason for the high concentration of urban poor settlements in the central and northern parts of the city is due to the concentration of major employment and business activities in the above areas since the city was established. In this context,

Table 1.1. Distribution of urban poor settlements by municipal districts in Colombo City

District	No. of settlements	%
District 1	276	17
District 2A	490	30
District 2B	412	26
District 3	229	14
District 4	153	9
District 5	54	4
Total	1,614	100

Source: Poverty Profile, City of Colombo, February 2002

two out of the six case studies of urban poor settlements have been selected from the Colombo North area as the current research study.

It has been observed that none of the past research studies carried out on public transport has focused on this social stratum to envisage the way its livelihood is sustained by the accessibility to public transport.

As a result, marginal areas in the city, such as urban poor settlements and many suburban areas of Colombo, have not been adequately served by from the city's public transport network. However, it can be argued that the availability and affordability of public transport is a decisive factor for economic enhancement, particularly of the urban poor. Therefore, the present study may be considered a timely investigation of the users' and providers' perceptions on the accessibility and quality of public transport operating in the City of Colombo.

1.4   Focus of the research project

The sustainable livelihoods approach can be used in understanding the complex relationships of the household assets base of the urban poor. In this context, public transport services can be seen as an important aspect that influences the asset base of urban poor communities by way of providing links to income earning opportunities. Reliable, easily accessible and affordable public transport would no doubt increase the mobility of the poor, whereby they could have access to income-earning opportunities. In this context, the main aim of the current research study is to find out the ways in which the access and quality of public transport would help improve the livelihoods of the urban poor. The research also aims at investigating the perspectives of the urban poor on public transport services as being the users of public transport, in order to ensure quality and accessibility aspects. Furthermore, the research project analyzes the partnerships under which public transport is currently provided in Colombo and in the country as a whole. This is because public transport services in Sri Lanka are currently provided by different parties, such as the government, public sector, private sector and individuals. These different arrangements have different impacts on the quality of and access to public transport. Therefore, it is of prime importance to study both the supply aspects and the user perspectives of public transport and their impacts on the livelihoods of the urban poor.

1.5   Research approach

A case-study-based participatory research approach has been adapted, using interviews and a series of focus group discussions at the urban poor settlement and city level, covering the key actors such as users, regulators and service providers. Six underserved settlements in and around Colombo were identified as case study locations. Interviews and discussions were held covering all prominent user categories, namely, male and female adults, male and female elderly and disabled persons, schoolgirls and schoolboys. Members of all the three racial groups, i.e. Sinhalese, Tamil and Muslims were included under each of these categories in order to ensure racial representation in the study.

Considering the availability of time, resources and the focus of the study, six urban poor settlements were identified in consultation with the research coordinator of WEDC, Loughborough University, UK, for the current research project. The basis for selecting the six settlements included representation of the different categories of urban poor settlements (i.e. slums, squatter and relocated low-income settlements), to represent the entire city and to include the different sizes of settlements in terms of numbers of households. The six settlements are thus fairly representative of the types, size and spread of the city's urban poor settlements, though are not based on a systematic sampling but purely on practical considerations and the informed judgment of the local research team.

The entire study was carried out taking **user perceptions** as the key focus. Partnerships of both public and private, and bus, rail and para-transport were covered. It was presumed that the people who use public transport almost daily, and the service providers who operate those services, might have better solutions to the problems they face. This study evolved on that basis, which was taken within the context of the sustainable livelihoods approach. The research project has been developed and carried out based on a literature review, historical overview, and an analysis of the current situation, case studies and focus group discussions.

1.6   Scope and limitations

The scope of the research was the urban public transport that covers the City of Colombo and its suburbs. Colombo is the commercial capital of the country and is the starting point of all major public transport routes. The study revealed that inter-provincial public transport is under the purview of the provincial councils, which may have their own procedures and mechanisms, as long as these are in line with the national policy framework. However, the study did not go into such detail, as its focus was the Colombo urban area. Within the Colombo area, the study paid attention to investigating issues relating to access and the quality of public transport through the key actors such as users, providers and regulators. The perspectives of the key actors were framed into issues and recommendations with a view to improving access to and quality of public transport.

1.7   Introduction to the research process

This section explains the process in which the research was conducted, the preparatory work involved and the reflections of the research team.

Since inception, Dr. Sohail Khan guided the research from the Loughborough University, UK. Through consultation among the research team, a framework of research was developed. Key actors and issues to be addressed were identified through consultation with relevant resource persons by the local research team. Checklists for interviewing key actors were prepared and tested through discussions and brainstorming sessions.

1.8   Working hypothesis

This research project was initiated based on the premise that public transport is one of the key aspects that broadens access to the available livelihood options by the urban poor. Within a specific situation, once options are available, people will make choices and then develop strategies to gain the desired ends. For the urban poor, these choices are comparatively few. The cost of each choice compels them to act so as to optimize their strategic actions. The 'location' factor thus becomes primarily important to them, as location is the key point of reference in terms of access to their basic activities and services such as employment, other informal income-generation activities, marketing, education, health and social networks. Public transport thus becomes a significant contribution to enhance the livelihood pattern of the urban poor by linking their location to services. In this context, there are some central questions, such as: How does public transport operate in the city? How accessible is it for the poor? How is it affordable? What is the quality of the services provided? remain to be answered. The present study attempts to investigate the pertinent issues of the above questions, and to find out appropriate answers by involving the key actors who are engaged in the process.

1.9   Research process

The research process, which is indicated below, was developed based on the broad research framework provided in the inception report. The key steps listed below were followed in carrying out the project.

Step 1:   Understanding the research premise and developing the research proposal to suit the local conditions in Colombo.

Step 2:   Identification of the type and depth of information and data required, based on the key issues, actors and processes involved.

Step 3:   Identification of the main sources of data and interviewees for the research through a review of the literature and personal contacts.

Step 4:   Developing the checklists for collection of the required data and information.

Step 5:   Carrying out a detailed literature survey.

Step 6:   Identification of urban poor settlements / communities for interviews based on the criteria developed under the study.

Step 7:   Identification of resource persons for the Project Advisory Committee.

Step 8:   Identification of field research staff and their recruitment in order to carry out field data collection.

Step 9:   Briefing for field research staff on the project and training them for carrying out the field research / informant interviews.

Step 10:   Carrying out a historical analysis relating to public transport using available literature and through interviews of relevant resource personnel.

Step 11:   Visits to the urban poor settlements identified, familiarization with the community. Informing the community leaders of the purpose of the research project and getting their help in identifying different categories of community members for interview (men, women, school children, disabled persons etc.).

Step 12:   Preparation of settlement profiles for each urban poor settlement identified, consisting of basic facts about the community, its location and size etc.

Step 13:   Interviewing the identified community members (elderly persons, the disabled, adult men, women, school children) of the urban poor settlements.

Step 14:   Interviewing other groups of public transport users (i.e. office workers and ordinary citizens).

Step 15:   Interviewing public transport providers (bus owners and representatives of owner's associations).

Step 16:   Interviewing operators of public transport (i.e. conductors and drivers).

Step 17:   Interviewing representatives of public transport regulatory agencies.

Step 18:   Carrying out focus group meetings of urban poor communities and provider groups to further strengthen the issues identified through the interviews and literature survey.

Step 19:   Conducting monthly Project Advisory Committee meetings to review the progress of the research study and to guide the research activities.

Step 20:   Synthesizing the information gathered through interviews.

Step 21:   Revisiting the field for verification of information

Step 22:   Translating the synthesized Sinhala version of information into English.

Step 23:   Computer processing of information.

Step 24:   Preparation of the draft research report.

Step 25:   Presentation of the draft report to the Project Coordinator at WEDC and to the Project Advisory Committee (PAC).

Step 26:   Incorporating the comments, if any, by the Project Coordinator and the PAC.

Step 27:   Preparation of the final research report.

Step 28:   Presentation of the research results at a national workshop in Colombo.

Step 29:   Incorporation of the findings of the workshop with the study.

Step 30:   Handing over the final research results to the Project Coordinator

Step 31:   Sharing the research findings with local interested groups such as academics, researchers and policymakers.

1.10   Limitations of the research process

The research process adopted was flexible in terms of its identification of key interviewees as well as urban poor communities. The process was not limited by statistical sampling or hypotheses; rather it paid much more attention to the interactions between and among the key actors of public transport services in Colombo. Therefore, with a view to better understanding the perspectives of different actors (i.e. the users, providers and regulators of public transport), a manageable sample of the key interviewees was chosen.

Interviews of community members of urban poor settlements were much easier than that of transport providers, operators and regulators who were busy with their day-to-day business. However, repeated visits and intermittent interviews were carried out in order to extract the required information from these categories. On the whole, the process of information gathering took a considerable amount of time (3 to 4 months), but enabled the research team to gather adequate data and information.

Most of the information was of a descriptive nature, which was analyzed based on key themes, issues and perspectives.

Section 2

Historical overview

2.1 Background

Sri Lankan society has been predominantly agriculture based throughout its 2,600-year history. Domesticated agro-crops (mainly paddy and highland crops) used to be cultivated through community-based efforts and were used mainly for local consumption. The associated accessibility needs of people and the social attitudes to transport sprang out of this socio-economic system. Goods used to be carried on people's heads or in makeshift litters; people were used to either walking for several kilometres or using bullock-carts for their transport needs. Distances were not great and speed was not a matter of great concern. Accordingly, the road network system consisted of footpaths and gravel roads.

A similar socio-economic structure continued during the early days of Sri Lanka's colonial era, which spanned nearly four and half centuries, from 1505 to 1948. However, especially during the 150 years of British occupation, the last span of the colonial period, a transition in the agro-based socio-economic system took place with the introduction of 'plantation-crops' such as tea, rubber and coconut. These crops were not for local consumption, but were to be *sold out* (exported out of the locality) for economic gain. While paddy and other domestic crops remained for local consumption, and the cultivation of which was not encouraged, every attempt was made to cultivate the plantation crops for over hundreds and thousands of acres. Firstly coffee and then tea were introduced to the central hill-country, clearing its thick forest cover. Rubber was concentrated mainly in the low-country wetlands and coconut was re-introduced as a plantation crop in the west, southwest and northwest coastal areas.

This socio-economic structure was more significant towards the latter part of the 19th century. The 'plantation economy' was creating a subtle change in the social attitudes and value systems on one hand, and on the other it was also creating a more visible change in the systems of transport. More speedy and efficient means of transport were required and thus new roads and railway lines were constructed—primarily to facilitate the production process and to transport the plantation products to Colombo from other major town centres. The basic skeleton of the present system of road and railway networks began to appear, a result of the prevalent socio-economic structure.

2.2 20th Century—up to 1957

The urban and regional physical settings of the country were transformed to cater to the needs of the plantation sector as it became established as the key aspect of the national economy. By early 20th century, the road and railway network had expanded further. Major railway lines: Badulla–Colombo, Kandy–Colombo, and the southern coastal line from Matara to Colombo were in operation. The railways were state-owned and were under the purview of the Ceylon Government Railway (C.G.R.), which was later known as Sri Lanka Railways.

Road transport also expanded, with the construction of many steel bridges across rivers and waterways. The first passenger car was introduced in 1902 and that the paved way to the construction of an all-weather road system. With the increasing mobility needs of the people, T.W. Collet started the first bus-cum-lorry service from Colombo to Chilaw in 1907, which was later extended up to Puttalam in 1910. This marked the formation of the first bus company in Sri Lanka, known as the 'Ceylon Motor Transit Company'.

At the same time, the growth of the City of Colombo coincided with the transformation of the socio-economic and physical contexts of the country, based as they were on the plantation sector. Historically, Colombo was famed for its port and related trade. Export of plantation crops and related trade activities, and the growth of light industries, however, created an unprecedented influx of workers into the city from all over the country in search of jobs. This unplanned growth gave rise to the early forms of slum settlements within the city. At first, these were over-crowded labour quarters, creating severe hygiene problems. Although there were some physical planning interventions by the pre- and post-independence regimes, the city continued to grow with its ever-increasing worker population; transport and other infrastructure networks were not well geared to cater to this fast population growth.

Within such national and urban contexts, provision of bus and rail services, too, continued with hardly any pro-active thinking. From time to time a number of Acts and Ordinances were enacted and commissions were appointed, but these nevertheless were always reactionary measures.

Based on Ranasinghe (1988:04–07), the key events that took place in the transport sector during the pre- and post- independence eras up to mid-1950s, and the salient features contained therein, are given in Table 1.

It is significant that during this entire period, bus services were under private entrepreneurs while rail services remained under government monopoly. Private sector dominance of bus services with no direct state intervention created intense rivalry and malpractices among the private bus companies who operated in the city. Independence from the British in 1948, too, made no impact on the direction or qualitative enhancement of transport services in the country.

By mid-1950s, entrepreneurs had formed limited liability companies within their regions of operation. There were 76 such companies in operation on a monopoly route permit basis, which was found to be unsatisfactory. The bus services and the government interventions had finally come to a stage where recommendations were made by the Sansoni Commission, appointed in 1954, to set up a Transport Board to advise and control private operators and establish a joint government/private bus corporation to provide services, starting with Colombo Municipal Council Areas.

Table 2.1. Key events in public transport—20th century up to nationalization of bus services

		Event	Salient features
PRE-INDEPENDENCE PERIOD		1891 Ceylon Government Railway Ordinance was enacted	• Ceylon Government Railway was formed. • Passenger and freight fares were decided, based on this ordinance.
		1907 First recorded omnibus operation in Sri Lanka, from Colombo to Chilaw by T.W. Collett	
		1916 Enactment of the Vehicle Ordinance Act No.4 of 1916	• Registration of motor vehicles and drivers by the Inspector General of Police. • The licensing authorities viz. the government agents and Chairmen of Local Authorities.
		The bus service to Kandy was introduced after World War II	
		1925 A commission, under the chairmanship of J. Strachan, Director of Public Works, was appointed	Purpose of this commission was to report: • on the means of transport already existing; and • to assist the government to formulate a policy for encouraging the economic development of the Island by roads, railways and waterways.
		1927 Motor Car Ordinance No.20 of 1927	• It amended and consolidated the law relating to motorcars. • Amended the Vehicle Ordinance No.4 of 1916. • Created the Department of the Registrar of Motor Vehicles on roads, including the insurance of vehicles. • However, it did not make any change with regard to the licensing authorities.
		1936 The number of buses in operation had increased to 2,500	• Intense rivalry and cutthroat competition among the bus operators were common. This led to unsafe driving practices and assaults. • Unequal distribution of routes, absence of timetables, lack of passenger comfort and safety were quite notable.
		1937 A Commission headed by F. D. Hammond was appointed to report on the Island's transport system	• Recommended to establish a central authority for all forms of transport.
		1938 Motor Car Ordinance No.45 of 1938 was enacted	• Provided for the Commissioner of Motor Transport with wider powers to be the sole Licensing Authority, Chief Examiner of Motor Cars, Head of Motor Traffic Advisory Board. • Provision was made for compulsory insurance against third party risks.
PRE-INDEPENDENCE PERIOD		Early 1940s	• Increase in passenger traffic and growth of investors in the bus industry led to intense rivalry among operators, poor productivity, law breaking and unsatisfactory levels of service. • Thus the Government engaged S.W. Nelson to re-organize the transport system of the Island, which led to the enactment of Omnibus Service Licensing Ordinance No.47 of 1942.
		1942 Omnibus Service Licensing Ordinance No.47 of 1942	• Advocated controlled territorial monopolies. • Brought about standardization of buses by way of regulation and control of the use of omnibuses on roads and exclusive road service licences for omnibus services. • Made relevant amendments to the Motor Car Ordinance No.45 of 1938. • Operators had to combine and transform themselves into limited liability companies.

Table 2.1. Continued

	Event	Salient features
POST-INDEPENDENCE PERIOD (UP TO 1957)	Post-World War II period	• Was marked by a steady decline in the railway's fortunes and also disorganized road transport. • Thus, D. R. Rutnam was appointed to survey the position of transport in Ceylon, with special reference to road and rail. He was expected to make recommendations about the wasteful competition, to formulate a plan of development and to suggest a framework of legislation to implement the recommendations.
	D.R. Rutnam Report	• With regard to passenger transport, Rutnam took the view that no co-ordination of road and rail was necessary. • Suggested establishing a Transport Board. • Recommended amending the Omnibus Service Licensing Ordinance No.17 of 1942. • Resulted in the enactment of Motor Traffic Act No.14 of 1951.
	1951 Motor Traffic Act No.14 of 1951	Made provisions for: • replacing the Commissioner of Motor Transport by a Commissioner of Motor Traffic; • placing the responsibility of issuing licences for motor vehicles and the collection of license fees on the Central Government; and • forming the bus companies into public (as opposed to private) limited liability companies before 1st January 1954.
POST-INDEPENDENCE PERIOD (UP TO 1957)	1954 Sansoni Commission	• Although the Motor Traffic Act No.14 of 1951 was intended to ensure successful operation of the public companies, this did not happen in practice. Thus the Governor Soulbury appointed a Commission headed by Waldor Sansoni on March 18, 1954 to: ➤ inquire and report on the omnibus companies and the improvements necessary for their proper operation in the public interest; ➤ investigate and report on the fare structure and recommend any revision considered necessary; and ➤ inquire and report on capital requirements to establish a public omnibus transport system and methods of forming it. • This commission was concerned only with bus operation; it studied in great deal the working of the existing system and dealt at length with individual bus companies. The main aspects it examined were: ➤ the Nelson Scheme of route operation; ➤ the adequacy of buses and services; ➤ the organization of bus companies; and ➤ the management and financial position of bus companies. • A technical adviser was also on the team to examine the standards of service, safety, repair and maintenance of buses. • The Commission recommended amendments to the Motor Traffic Act, reorganization of the Motor Traffic Department and the formation of a Transport Board. • The report of the Sansoni Commission stated that between 1948 to 1953 the number of omnibuses licensed increased from 1,502 to 2,560 and passengers carried per month from 11,891,000 to 23,915,000. • The bus service supplied by 76 public bus companies and other operators on a monopoly route permit basis was not considered satisfactory in the 1950s. The bus operators, meanwhile, wanted to increase passenger fares. • In its report the Commission recommended the setting up of a Transport Board to advise and control private operators and the establishment of a joint government/private bus corporation to provide services, starting with Colombo Municipal Council Areas.

2.3   Nationalization of bus services and their operation up to 1977

After independence from the British on 4th February 1948, the first significant change in the socio-political situation of the country took place with the formation of a new government in 1956. The nationalization of bus services, too, coincided with this change.

The government appointed three committees—one local, another from the London Transport Executive and the third from Germany—to study the ways in which nationalization should take place. All three committees recommended a phased take over of the private bus companies. Nevertheless, the government decided to nationalize the whole passenger transport industry in one go under Act No.48 of 1957, which established the Ceylon Transport Board. Accordingly, on the 1st January 1958, the Ceylon Transport Board (CTB) undertook the provision of passenger services throughout the country.

As Diandas (1988:88) explains, nationalization of bus services into a single undertaking (the CTB) brought many changes. These included linking bus routes into planned networks, especially in the cities, extension of services into remote rural areas, operating urban buses late into the night, the introduction of ticket machines, an improved (for a time) indication of destinations and provision of bus shelters. Operational output improved up to the level of 250km per bus per day, compared to the monopoly companies' performance of 160km per bus per day. In addition, creation of new bus depots and service stations all over the country, provision of a common wage system and an employee provident fund for the workers, along with other welfare facilities, were introduced to make the public transport an efficient government undertaking.

Diandas (1988:90–92) explains that the success of the CTB was mainly threefold. Firstly, it brought into management a mix of management types—a few outside experts, government servants and managers of the bus companies, all untarnished by ownership interests. Secondly, the workforce was comparatively satisfied and motivated, with better working conditions and the necessary skills training. Thirdly, a new fleet of 1,000 or more buses, designed for passenger transport, were bought; this was later followed by a gift of 1,000 double-decker buses from London Transport.

From 1958 to 1976, the daily-operated bus fleet increased from 2,318 to 4,600 and the yearly travel distance in kilometres increased from 165 million to 398 million. By 1968, the CTB had been transformed into a profit-making public sector institution. However, soon after it showed the signs of downturn, mainly due an unnecessary political interference. As a service-oriented venture, the CTB was lenient about increasing its fares. Furthermore, an increase in bus fares was a highly political decision, as the Government would not dare to face the subsequent public outcry. Thus, cost escalations, especially after the oil crisis in 1973, were not compensated for by equivalent fare increases. Also, a host of other reasons started contributing to the CTB's decline in the early 1970s. Diandas (1988:92) sums up three key factors:

i.   disillusionment of management, the workforce, the public, press and the government;

ii. financial problems; and

iii. increasing political interference by way of adding unnecessary numbers to the workforce and interfering in management decisions.

Diandas (1988), cited earlier, also takes the view that the government did not accept that urban bus services required tax support. Instead, the losses incurred were cited as mere signs of inefficiency.

The cumulative effect of all this was the CTB's escalating heavy losses for several years. By 1975, it was neither in a position to add new buses to its fleet nor to meet the increasing running costs. Overcrowding became worse than ever. Petty political interferences forced an indiscriminate intake of unwanted staff and turned the CTB into a grossly mismanaged institution.

However, during this period the private sector was not allowed to operate passenger transport on a regular basis. Private operators were allowed to operate taxi services, especial buses and vans for excursions, and so on. The individuals using cars and motorcycles were also limited due to import resections and the high cost of vehicles. However, non-motorized transport modes, such as pedal cycles etc., were in operation in addition to the government-dominated passenger bus transport.

The economic structure of the country saw little change up to this time. The plantation sector was still the key source of national income, while the agricultural sector of the country was getting high government patronage. Self-sufficiency in paddy production— a historical achievement during the pre-colonial era that nevertheless lost its momentum during the British rule—was yet to be re-achieved. The physical development of the country as a whole had been gradual, while in Colombo it was comparatively more significant. Port-related activities, government offices, government bank headquarters and a few private enterprises were concentrated in Colombo, making it attractive for both white- and blue-collar jobs. An increasing demand for better passenger transport services was generated in both urban and rural areas, due to gradual increases in economic activities and increases in the population.

2.4   Formation of a new government in 1977

By 1977, the country had slipped into an economic downturn and at the general election of 1977 a new government came to power. This change witnessed a major shift of national economic policies towards opening up the economy and making the private sector actively participate in the mainstream development process.

The CTB was under severe strain during this period because the demand for travel had shot up by 17 per cent by 1978. The government, overseeing the situation based on its open economic policy, resorted to two remedies to face this situation—regionalization and deregulation of passenger transport services (Diandas:1994:05). The CTB was decentralized by Act No.19 in 1978, to form nine Regional Transport Boards (RTBs), one for each province, and establishing the Sri Lanka Central Transport Board (SLCTB). The SLCTB's main responsibilities were to co-ordinate the supplies, inter-regional services, heavy repairs, to procure sufficient new buses, to deal with overcrowding and numerous trade –union-related issues. Under deregulation, private buses were allowed to operate again providing passenger transport, exactly 20 years after the nationalization of public transport.

2.5   Re-emergence of private buses

After two decades of nationalization, in 1979, the government decided to permit private bus owners to operate regular services on all routes in complement and/or compete with the RTB buses. By 1980, there were around 5000 private buses in operation. These were allowed to operate on the routes of their choice, which were invariably the profitable ones, and often in conflict with the cash strapped RTB operations.

The decision to allow private buses to operate again was based on the following presumptions:

i.   private buses would relieve the RTBs' inability to cope with demand, and would thus complement the RTB services;

ii. the Treasury would be relieved of its burden of massive annual allocations to purchase new buses and spare parts to meet with the demand; and thus,

iii. the government would be relieved of public criticism and passengers would no longer suffer difficulties with travel.

This move had the immediate effect of easing passenger travel needs; nevertheless the decision to allow private buses to re-operate seems rather ad hoc and an apparent last resort. It lacked pre-planning on how the private buses would operate or on how they would co-operate with the RTB buses.

The consequences of the lack of pre-planning were evident immediately. There was no central body to manage and control the private buses' affairs. Initially no tickets were issued. No standards were specified on the size, capacity or internal dimensions of the private buses. As a result they appeared in all sizes and types. In the meantime, the government liberalized the import of motor coaches. Eventually, reconditioned vans and mini-coaches of small and medium sizes and with low roofs etc. were used for passenger transport with no regulations at all. Most of these were not designed for public transport—there were no bells or bars to hold on to and aisles were occupied by folding seats, causing passenger discomfort.

For these private buses, parking spaces or terminals, at least of a rudimentary nature, had not been thought of. They were allowed to operate at will, and obviously opted for most the profitable routes, which were also the ones with the highest passenger demand. There was no apparent necessity to stop at the designated bus-stops to pick up or drop off passengers. Instead the private buses stopped anywhere along the routes for passengers. There were no timetables and, therefore, the private buses mostly operated during peak hours. There was no reliability of services. Often private buses competed with the RTB buses—as a result, cowboy driving, racing or hanging back for a bus load increased traffic; anarchy on roads became common. However, private buses were not allowed to take higher fares than what was determined by the government for the RTB buses.

By the early 1980s, Colombo had grown into the country's most densely populated urban centre. Open economic policies and the intensified agglomerated economies increased employment opportunities within the city and thus there was a massive daily commuter population into the city from all over the country. Colombo port was transforming into a major container-handling port in the South Asian region. There was always a demand for unskilled or semi-skilled labour, and thus urban low-income settlements continued to grow, amounting to half of Colombo's population. A heavy inflow of vehicles began to cause traffic problems at peak hours, to which the private buses of all kinds were contributing significantly. Road networks and other infrastructure were not developing to keep pace with the additional vehicles on the roads. Road accidents were on the increase.

The government soon realized the need to bring in controlling measures to the private bus operation, and in April 1981 a separate Ministry of Private Omnibus Transport was established to administer and supervise the private omnibus sector.

In December 1981, the Minister of Private Omnibus Transport appointed a committee under the chairmanship of A.C.M. Ameer to recommend the establishment of suitable machinery for regulating, controlling and supervising the operation of private omnibus services and the necessary legal requirements for its implementation. In addition, the committee was asked to report on improvements that were necessary for the orderly growth of the private omnibus industry, with special reference to prevent the wasteful duplication of facilities with other existing forms of transport.

The recommendations of the Ameer Committee were contained in the Private Omnibus Services Act No.44 of 1983. Accordingly, in January 1984 a separate Department of Private Omnibus Transport was established with a director to administer the Act, which later was amended as per Act No.38 of 1985.

Between 1979 and 1985, the number of private buses became double the number of RTB buses. Yet most of them were under 30-seat capacity. Ranasinghe (1988:105–107) summarizes the findings of a survey on the private bus sector carried out in 1986. Some key factors relevant to this study are cited below.

- 85 per cent of the seat capacity in private omnibus transport was provided by buses with 30 seats or less; of this, 31 per cent was provided by even smaller buses with less than 19 seats.

- The private bus sector was dominated by one-bus owners. About 94 per cent of the operators owned only one bus each; such owners owned 87 per cent of all the buses.

- 85 per cent of the private buses were not new, but imported reconditioned vehicles.

- Most of the owners had bought their buses partly with borrowed money, and of these 88 per cent had been borrowed from finance companies on hire purchase schemes.

- 56 per cent of the owners had been in the private omnibus service for two years or less.

- 85 per cent of the conductors were 25 years of age or less, while only 1 per cent were 40 years or less.

- 13 per cent of the drivers were 25 years or less, while 19 per cent were 40 years or less.

- 75 per cent of the conductors and 34 per cent of the drivers were unmarried.

- 62 per cent of the employees cited unemployment as the principle reason for joining bus transport generally, but only 32 per cent gave this as the primary reason for joining the private bus service.

- No employee reported that the Employee's Provident Fund (EPF) was paid on his behalf by his employer.

- It did not appear that owners were making a big profit out of their venture.

2.6 A review of the public transport sector (after the re-emergence of private buses, up to the late 80s)

The re-emergence of private buses brought instant relief to some of the long-stagnated transport issues, such as easing the overcrowding, reducing waiting times etc., and reducing heavy government budgetary allocations to support the CTB, which was running at a loss. Yet, the unplanned nature of the introduction brought about many other issues. After just six years of operation, the private bus industry was already in a shaky state. While bus fares were kept low, the operational costs of buses were rocketing, without any government intervention to provide tax concessions etc. Thus on the one hand, private operations did not appear to be making substantial profits, and on the other, passenger dissatisfaction was mounting with the services they were getting.

The effect of the re-introduction of private buses on the RTBs was also substantial. RTB buses were engaged in a 'losing battle with private buses. The private buses outnumbered the RTB buses and also they did not have to run within a scheduled timetable. Thus, on most routes, the private buses ran ahead of the RTB buses, absorbing a major share of the passengers. Most popular routes were fully dominated by the private buses. The RTBs did not have any strategy to counter this new situation, the cumulative effect of which was the steady depletion of daily income for RTB buses amidst rising costs.

The most important aspect of this whole scene was that the passengers were also in dilemma. They were still far from getting reasonable transport services. The RTBs had been service-oriented; during the era of their monopoly it was also part of state responsibility to provide transport services at off-peak hours, late at night, on remote routes etc. However, with the introduction of private buses, the RTBs cut back on these responsibilities. With decreasing income and, therefore, increasing losses, and less government patronage, the RTBs were also not in a position to add more buses to run on such routes and at such times. Private buses, on the other hand were not interested running on less profitable routes and during off-peak hours. Therefore, the passengers were not getting the services they used to get.

Colombo was fast being transformed as the major urban metropolis, with increased population densities. Agglomeration economies continued and the daily commuter population was growing. Slum and squatter dwellers represented half of the city's population. They occupied rail reservation lands, low-lying areas and other vacant lands, which were close to junctions and town centres where employment was most accessible.

Liberalized economic policies led to a thriving private sector. The monopoly of the plantation sector as the key source of national revenue was now facing competition from light industries concentrated in the free-trade zones, the garment industry and from the revenue brought in by a massive outgoing workforce to the Middle Eastern countries as housemaids and semi-skilled personnel. In addition to the conventional jobs found in Colombo, the low-income groups concentrated in slum and squatter settlements were highly attracted to the Middle Eastern job market. Open economic policies had a significant impact on social attitudes and value systems within a few years. Money flew into the hands of people from a variety of sources. Television was introduced to Sri Lankan society, which was fast being transformed into a consumer society. This trend was much faster in Colombo and other urban areas than in the rural settings. Associated social issues were also visible. Drugs, such as heroin, began to appear. Slum and squatter dwellers were more susceptible to this menace for a variety of reasons.

These complex socio-economic transformations were, in turn, reflected in people's attitudes towards transport and their increasing transport needs, which spanned into different times of the day. With the increased pace of life, time became more an issue of concern. However, public transport was not geared to address these demands. School buses operated by the CTB and then the RTBs, at a very concessionary rate, were fast diminishing. All this created a demand for para-transport modes on a significant scale. Trishaws imported from India were arriving on the roads, filling the gap in public transport. Some people resorted to chartered school/work vans. Motorcycles were fast replacing bicycles. Liberalizing the import of motor coaches had also brought all kinds of vehicles onto roads, and increased traffic congestion and accidents, especially in urban areas. Air pollution rates were on the increase, which had recently become considered an important aspect in the city environment.

The road network of Colombo and its suburbs, along with other infrastructure, were also not expanding to cope with the increasing traffic. Therefore, heavy traffic at junctions was quite common. Galle Road, which had the highest traffic density, was almost impassable during peak hours. Similar traffic congestion was common elsewhere. Closure of roads at some points due to security measures since the mid-1980s worsened the situation on the city roads.

All the parties responsible for public transport—the government, the policymakers, the RTBs, the private bus operators and even the passengers—were caught up in a situation to which no one had a clear answer. This was rather strange because the demand for public transport was rising throughout. Nevertheless, there was no well-co-ordinated plan of action to capitalize on this demand and provide the passengers with better transport.

By late 80s, the political situation of the country too was in turmoil. The civil war in the North and East and the youth uprising in the South had taken their toll. After a brief peak during 1978–82, the country's economy started going through a difficult period, especially towards the late 80s. The government brought forward the devolution of political and administrative powers to the provincial level as a solution to the country's political problems, and that action had impacts on the transport sector as well.

2.7   Devolution up to the present

Closer and more active involvement of the people in decision-making, development of local talent and dispersal of governmental processes were among the key objectives of the devolution of power that took place, along with the 13th amendment to the Constitution, in 1987. However, it took some years for the country's administrative setting to adjust accordingly. Provincial Council elections were held much later in 1991, and eight Provincial Councils were formed covering the nine provinces. These were vested with the powers to promote, establish and engage in agricultural, industrial, commercial and trading enterprises and other income-generating projects within each province.

The transport sector took a new direction in line with this devolution package. First and foremost, the devolution of control over bus services was shifted from the central government to provincial governments, viz. to the Provincial Ministry of Transport. Portfolios with ministerial positions, similar to those of the central government were created in these provincial governments. However, each minister had a number of portfolios under his or her purview and thus, a separate officer or an authority was established. For instance, in the Western Province Provincial Council, a separate authority, the Western Province Road Passenger Transport Authority, was established with a full-time Chairman and Chief Executive and in other provincial councils, a Director of Transport or an officer bearing a similar designation, administered the operation of public transport within the province.

2.8   'Peoplization' of RTBs

As mentioned earlier, although the constitutional changes were made to devolve power through provincial councils in 1987, it took some more years before they came into operation. By this time, one notable change had occurred. All the 92 bus depots belonging to the RTBs were dissolved and converted into oddly termed 'Peoplized' Transport Companies, as per Act No.23 of 1987. Employees themselves were made part of the ownership and management of these companies, by selling 50 per cent of shares to them with the rest held by the Treasury. Thus the responsibility for administration and management of these companies was transferred to the employees themselves, in an effort to get rid of unwanted political interference and make the operation more viable.

2.9   National Transport Commission (NTC)

Along with the devolution of power and formation of provincial ministries and authorities, the National Transport Commission was established as the agency of the Ministry of Transport and Highways by Act 37 of 1991. Its principal functions included advising the government on policy, regulating inter-provincial bus services, guiding and assisting provincial transport authorities on policy etc.

Within a few years, the effect of 'Peoplization' was visible. Disintegration of small depots led to uncontrolled competition among themselves. Income diminished even more and the resources began to be underutilized. Thus, as per Act No.30 of 1996, the 'Peoplized' depots were amalgamated into 11 Companies, under the Companies Act No.17 of 1982.

2.10   A brief overview

The situation of the public transport sector did not seem to improve with the events that took place along with the devolution of powers to provincial level or the formation of various authorities. None of these organizations grasped the crux of the issue or perceived the scenario holistically. All subsections of public transport—the private buses, the 'Peoplized' bus companies, the railway, the road and rail infrastructure—were faced with increasing problems and continued to run at a loss (except for the private buses). The reasons for this primarily related to poor management of public transport operations and the difficulty they had facing the competition created by the private sector bus owners. By contrast, the private bus owners (operating mostly as individually-owned business activities) operated only on profitable routes and in peak hours to make their profits. The government-owned buses, while loosing income, were required to operate as a service that the people expected the government to provide. This complex situation has lead to an unorganized, inefficient public transport system existing in Colombo and in Sri Lanka.

Devolution, giving autonomy to each provincial council to decide on its own transport sector, led to further disintegration of the system as a whole, mainly due to a lack of co-ordination and overlapping of certain functions. Diandas (1994:33–43) cites that devolution has made no or little contribution on such aspects as scheduling and over-supply (of private buses), enforcement of standards and improvement and maintenance of bus stations, stands and terminals. Nor has it addressed the prolonged issues of over-crowding, safety and comfort etc. on the part of the passengers. In fact most of these issues were central to the transport sector and had nothing much to do with devolution.

Thus, in 1996, funded by the World Bank, a study was made by a joint World Bank/ Government of Sri Lanka team, with a view to recommending a strategic framework for the improvement of public transport. This study put forward recommendations on policy reorientation, improving efficiency of public investments, transport infrastructure provisions and environmental and social sustainability. However, it was revealed that the above strategy document remains a study; no use has been made of it for any significant changes in transport policy and strategy. The reason for this is that the policymakers at the ministry level seem to have not made proposals to the government for implementation of any such recommendations.

City level transport related information

Population trends

Population data for the city of Colombo is available starting from the first population census in 1871, up to 2001. Accordingly, the total residential population, average population density and the growth rate are indicated in the following table.

Table 2.2. The area, population density and the population growth rate,
City of Colombo (1871–2001)

Census	Extent (Ha)	Population	Density (P/Ha)	Growth rate
1871	2448.6	98,847	40	-
1881	2448.6	110,509	45	1.18
1891	2448.6	126,825	52	1.48
1901	2720.6	154,691	56	2.20
1911	3091.1	211,274	68	3.66
1921	3350.3	224,163	73	0.61
1931	3368.4	284,155	84	2.67
1946	3438.4	362,074	105	1.83
1953	3593.9	425,081	118	2.48
1963	3710.4	511,639	138	2.04
1971	3711.0	562,430	152	1.24
1981	3711.0	587,647	158	0.45
2001	3729.0	642,020	172	0.46

Source: 1. Centenary Volume, CMC, 1963
2. City of Colombo—Development Plan, Urban Development Authority, 1996
3. Census of Population, 2001

According to the above table it is evident that Colombo's population increased twofold within a 40-year period, from its first census in 1871 to 1911. This trend continued and by the 1953 population census Colombo had doubled its population again. However, the following 49 years, from 1953 to 2001, shows a relatively low population increase with the total population rising only from 425,081 in 1953 to 642,000 in 2001. This slow growth is reflected in the annual population growth rate figures, too, which recorded a rate of growth below 1 per cent per annum during the last two decades.

This slow population growth rate in the city may be considered a stabilization of city's residential population. Although the city's residential population stands at around 642,000 at present, the daily commuting population has shown a steady increase over the past few years. This commuting population was estimated by the Colombo Municipal Council as being 400,000 people per day during the year 2001. Thus the city of Colombo has grown to one million in size. When analyzing the population changes that are occurring in the city, there is a corresponding population increase occur in adjoining municipal and urban areas of Colombo, such as Kotte Municipal area, Dehiwala Mt. Lavinia Municipal area and several other urban and suburban council areas. However, it is worthy noting that the primacy of the city of Colombo as the capital city continues as the second largest city to Colombo, which is Dehiwala Mt. Lavinia, still had a residential population of only 209,787 as of 2001.

Land use pattern in the City of Colombo

According to the land use surveys carried out by the Urban Development Authority (UDA) of Sri Lanka, which is the principle planning authority, the changing pattern of land use in Colombo over the years is indicated in the following table.

Table 2.3. Land use distribution in the City of Colombo

Activity / Land Use	Extent (Ha)					
	Year 1977	&	Year 1996	%	Year 2010	%
Residential	1087	45.02	1402	37.60	1120	30.03
Commercial	201	5.60	225	6.03	375	10.06
Industrial	465	12.50	411	11.02	280	7.51
Cultural	-	-	249	6.68	260	6.97
Transport & utilities	610	16.30	983	26.36	745	19.98
Port related	-	-	-	-	560	15.02
Vacant & non-urban uses	142	3.60	262	7.03	186	4.99
Other	477	12.07	48	1.28	93	2.49
Total	3733	100.00	3729	100.00	3729	100.00

Source: City of Colombo Plan, Urban Development Authority (UDA)

According to the land use data available for 1977, 1996 and estimates for 2010, it is evident that residential land use continues to dominate the city's land use pattern. The second major category of land use is transport and utility services. Industries and commercial services occupy third and fourth ranks respectively in land use distribution. The important factor, which is not reflected in the land use distribution, is that many of the services and commercial establishments located in the city cater for the demand created within the Colombo region, as well as for demand from the entire country. Thus, the city's activity pattern attracts customers from different parts of the country, making it the busiest city centre in Sri Lanka.

Personal vehicle ownership trends

Vehicle ownership, as indicated in the Colombo Urban Transport Study of 1999, has been steadily increasing in the Colombo District from 1975 to around 1998. The vehicle ownership rate in the entire country is increasing only slowly It was farbelow 50 vehicles per 1000 of the population in 1975, reached about 40 vehicles per 1000 people in 1990 and was up to 74 vehicles per 1000 people in 1998. The situation in Colombo District is quite different from that of the country situation. In Colombo vehicle ownership passed 50 vehicles per 1000 of the population in 1980, and had further increased up to 100 vehicles per 1000 people in 1990. By 1998 vehicle ownership was close to 150 vehicles per 1000 of the population. Though vehicle ownership data is not available for Colombo for the entire period, the data for 1995 shows that the city had a vehicle ownership rate of between 200–250 vehicles per 1000 population, and had increased beyond 250 vehicles per 1000 population by 1998.Thus, it can be clearly understood that Colombo has the highest vehicle ownership rate per 1000 of the population when compared to Colombo District and Sri Lanka.

The vehicle ownership per capita by different types of vehicles is presented in the following table.

Table 2.4. Vehicle ownership per capita (1998)

Area	Estimated vehicle ownership (per 1000 people)	Ownership Level by Vehicle Type				
		Motor cycles	Three-wheelers	Cars & vans	Freight	Buses
CMC	262	66 (25%)	31 (12%)	113 (43%)	45 (17%)	8 (03%)
Colombo District	141	45(32%)	16 (11%)	56(40%)	20(14%)	4 (03%)
CMR	97	40 (41%)	9 (09%)	32 (33%)	13 (13%)	3 (03%)
Sri Lanka	74	38 (51%)	2 (03%)	21 (29%)	12 (16%)	1 (02%)

Source: Colombo Urban Transport Study—Stage 2, undertaken by W/S Atkins International, UK

The data available for 1998 shows that within Colombo Municipal Council area (CMC) the estimated vehicle ownership was 262 per 1000 people. The figure for Colombo District was 141 vehicles per 1000 of the population while for the entire country in 1998 the ownership rate was 74 vehicles per 1000 of the population. In terms of different types of vehicles, Colombo represents the highest per capita ownership rate of all the types of vehicles over other areas of Sri Lanka. It was evident, however, that cars and vans represent the highest percentage of vehicles (43 per cent) owned by people when compared to motorcycles, three-wheelers, buses and freight vehicles within the city of Colombo.

Modal split of daily trips made by each mode of transport

According to the Master Plan for Development of Transport in the Colombo Metropolitan Region, the daily flow of vehicles at the city boundary points and the split by mode of transport are as presented in the table below. The data represent the situation in 1995.

Table 2.5. Daily flow of vehicles at the city boundary points (1985)

Corridor (location)	Passengers per Day				Road Vehicles per Day		
	Bus	Private	Railway	Total	Bus	Private	Total
Galle Road (Dehiwela Bridge) / Coast line	187,881	82,154	61,000	331,035	5,834	34,612	40,446
	57%	25%	18%		14%	86%	
Negambo Rd (Victoria Bridge) / Puttalam line	146,019	82,597	8,000	236,616	3,816	37,461	41,277
	62%	35%	3%		9%	91%	
Kandy Rd (New Kelani Bridge) / Main line	205,534	77,785	88,000	371,319	5,251	35,203	40,454
	55%	21%	24%		1,3%	87%	
Ratnapura Rd (Kirullapone Bridge) / KV line	142,830	54,981	8,000	205,811	3,994	24,280	28,274
	69%	27%	4%		14%	86%	
Cotta Rd / SJ Pura Rd (Rajagiriya)	115,341	133,659		249,000	4,095	12,826	16,921
	46%	54%			24%	76%	
Horana Rd (Pamankada Bridge)	61,826	64,742		126,568	1,684	28,324	30,008
	49%	51%			6%	94%	
Kolonnawa Rd (Rail crossing)	45,651	13,845		59,496	1,022	7,262	8,284
	77%	23%			12%	88%	
Narahenpita Rd (Canal)	7,764	27,143		34,907	282	13,033	13,315
	22%	78%			2%	98%	
Low level Rd (Rail crossing)	40,628	23,271		63,899	1,106	10,214	11,320
	64%	36%			10%	90%	
Total	953,474	560,177	165,000	1,678,651	27,084	203,215	230,299
	57%	33%	10%		12%	88%	

Source: Colombo Urban Transport Study—Stage 2 undertaken by W/S Atkins International, UK

According to the above table, it is evident that the city of Colombo receives daily traffic flows from nine transport corridors, which connect the Colombo Metropolitan Region, as well as the more remote regions of Sri Lanka, with Colombo city. The total passenger inflow into the city was mainly via the buses (accounting for 57 per cent of daily passengers) while 33 per cent was via private vehicles. Railway passengers constitute the smallest of the three modes, being only 10 per cent of total passenger volume. In terms of the road vehicles, the daily inflow pattern shows a clear dominance of private vehicles (i.e. 88 per cent of the total vehicles), whereas buses account for only 12 per cent of the total.

The above data clearly indicates that passengers have been mainly depending on bus transport. Despite this, it is the private vehicles that dominate the city's vehicular population.

Estimated number of people employed in the transport sector

Data is not available on employment patterns in the city of Colombo by different sectors. The labour force and socio economic survey data for 1994 of the Department of Census and Statistics provides information for the district-level composition only (the district is a larger administrative area which includes both urban and rural areas). The following table was extracted from the data available in the Colombo Metropolitan Region Structure Plan Volume III data profile in 1998, and represents the Colombo District and Colombo Metropolitan Region situation with respect to the distribution of employment by different sectors.

Table 2.6. Sectoral clarification of employed labour force

Sector	Sri Lanka	Percentage of total	Colombo Metropolitan Region	Percentage of total	Colombo District	Percentage of total
Agriculture, fishing & forestry	2,036,035	40.6	171,354	15.3	29,192	04.3
Mining	62,674	01.3	9,032	0.8	3,925	0.6
Manufacturing	769,900	15.4	-	-	164,925	24.3
Electricity and gas	22,861	0.5	11,331	01.0	5,686	0.8
Construction	235,711	04.7	106,208	09.4	45,411	06.7
Wholesale	565,873	11.3	259,241	23.0	136,881	20.2
Transport	217,157	04.3	111,095	09.8	52,579	07.7
Insurance & banking services	85,583	01.7	54,352	04.8	34,438	05.1
Community services	817,367	16.3	366,356	32.5	187,051	27.6
Other	195,725	03.9	37,726	03.4	18,704	02.7
Total	5,008,886	100.0	1,126,695	100.0	678,793	100.0

Source: Adapted from the Colombo Metropolitan Regional Structure Plan—Volume III Data Profile, 1998, Urban Development Authority, Sri Lanka

As per the above table, it is evident that the proposition of employment provided by the transport sector is significantly low at the national level (4.3 per cent), and was about 7.7 per cent at Colombo District level. The Colombo Metropolitan region (which covers three administrative districts of Colombo, Kalutara and Gampaha) is the most urbanized region of Sri Lanka, yet represents only 9.8 per cent employment in the transport sector. Although there is no city-level data for Colombo city, it can be assumed that employment in the transport sector would be around 10 per cent of total employment when looking at the above data for the rest of the country.

Section 3

Current situation analysis

As part of the Annual Report (year 2000) of the Central Bank of Sri Lanka, the transport sector was discussed under broad categories such as bus transport (public and private), rail transport, civil aviation and port services. However, for the purposes of current study, which emphasizes passenger transport, bus transport and rail transport are considered more relevant than other categories. In addition to the above, some key modes of transport, such as three-wheelers, school vans, office vans and motorcycles, are used by people, particularly in urban areas, and are not reflected in the above report. The institutional arrangements and operational aspects of these transport modes vary according to where in the country they are. In the case of Colombo and its suburbs, where there is a highly concentrated urban population, an equally high percentage of modes of passenger transport operate. The main constraint to a discussion on these different modes of transport has been the lack of data, particularly on three-wheelers, school vans and office vans, which are being operated mostly on an individual basis with no proper authority for control and regulation.

3.1 Bus transport (public)

Currently, the public bus transport system in Sri Lanka is decentralized and handled at a provisional level. There are eight provincial councils covering the nine provinces of the country. The former Ceylon Transport Board (CTB) has thus been restructured to function as Regional Transport Companies (RTCs), sharing assets and the responsibilities of the regional bus companies among its employees and the state. The state sector retains only 50 per cent of the shares of the RTCs, while the balancing 50 per cent has been distributed among the employees.

Public bus transport at present attracts only about 44 per cent of daily passenger kilometres, while the balance is taken up by private sector transport operators. The objective of breaking the government's monopoly in public transport was to provide a better service to the public, while at the same time improving management of public transport. However, the biggest challenge faced by the public bus transport sector today is the unregulated competition by the private bus operators, particularly with regard to allocation of routes and time schedules.

The National Transport Commission (NTC), which is responsible for interprovincial transport, has prepared separate business plans for the 11 RTCs and a consolidation plan for all the RTCs with a view to improving their operation efficiency. According to the estimates of the RTCs, they need to operate at least 6,590 buses per day to provide a satisfactory service (this means an additional 1,000 buses should be provided to the RTCs for daily operation). This reveals that the public sector bus transport service (popularly known as CTB buses) is far below that of the private sector buses, which attracts 56 per cent of daily passenger kilometres.[1] As a result, as has been mentioned elsewhere in this report, most of the profitable routes are totally dominated by the private buses, leaving the unprofitable routes to the RTC buses. This unregulated competition has lead to a sharp decline in the RTC bus services.

3.2 Bus transport (private)

Starting from the early 1980s, private bus transport services have taken over a major share of passenger transport demand in the country (56 per cent of passenger kilometres). Motivated by profit, the private bus transport operators have gradually taken over most of the profitable routes. The private bus operators were operating legally as individual owners until 1996. However, the government introduced the formation of private bus companies in the year 2000 under the National Transport Act of 1996. The minimum requirement for the formation of a private bus company (which functions as a co-operative of private bus owners in a particular area) is that it organizes 50 buses in a particular geographical area. By end of year 2000, there were ten such companies formed in seven districts in the country. This implies there is still a large majority of private bus owners operating on an individual basis. The Provincial Road Passenger Transport Authority (PRPTA), which should be formed under each provincial council, regulates the operation of private bus transport services in their respective provinces. The first PRPTA was formed in the western province of Sri Lanka (where the capital city of Colombo is situated) in 1995. The 'regulations under the western provincial road passenger carriage services statue No.1 of 1992 and as amended by statue No.3 of 1993 and No.7 of 1995' was gazetted in 1996. The regulations in the above law provide the authority with powers and functions to control and regulate all the private passenger transport services within the province by PRPTA.

However, the regularization and control of the unregulated private bus transport system (since 1998 up until the late 1990s) has been an extremely difficult task. This seems to have been particularly difficult due to the operation of private buses on an individual basis. The government's effort to form private bus companies was considered the only way of controlling the operation of private bus services. The Annual Report (2000) of the Central Bank of Sri Lanka states that 'the private bus operators, though they provide a greater part of the service, are still faced with a number of problems which need to be resolved early if they are to improve the standards of their services. Non-availability of bus stations and parking spaces, lack of co-ordination between the private and public bus operations for allocation of routes and time schedules, poor road conditions, untrained crews and revenue leakage are the main problems.' Thus, it was clear that the introduction of private bus companies alone would not solve the complex problems associated with passenger transport in Sri Lanka.

Although the government was unable to regulate private bus operations, including provision of the necessary infrastructure, private sector domination has become inevitable in the competition with the government owned Regional Transport Company buses. The reason for this is that the private sector buses operate mainly as individual business activities with low operating costs. The leasing companies and banks provide lending facilities for the purchase of buses, the service crew can be employed on a low wage and the buses operate with no strict timetable, which means they can mainly target peak hours where they can earn more.

---

1.   The World Bank, Sri Lanka Transport Sector Strategy, August 1996

3.3 Rail transport

Rail transportation in Sri Lanka is handled by Sri Lanka Railways (SLR), which is a state-owned monopoly. The SLR is a government department, which provides railway passenger and freight transport services in the country. The contribution of Sri Lanka Railways to passenger transport has always been less significant than bus and private vehicle transportation. Due to an increasing shift in freight transport away from railways and towards the roads has also caused a sharp decline in goods transportation by rail since the early 1990s. As has been described by the Annual Report of the Central Bank, issues such as late arrivals, overcrowded compartments and a low degree of safety and comfort are some of the pertinent problems faced by an average train traveller. On the other hand, the Sri Lanka Railway has made efforts to tackle these problems, given its limited resources, outdated rolling stock, weak rail tracks and outdated signalling system, particularly since the late 1990s.

Considering the important role played by Sri Lanka Railway in the area of passenger and freight transport, several projects have been implemented to improve its conditions and performance, particularly during the late 1990s. These improvements have mainly concentrated in and around the Colombo region so as to cater for rising demand in that area.

Being state-owned, railway transport offers people many concessionary services. These include monthly season tickets for office workers and passes valid for three months on a pre-paid basis for school children at a cheaper rate than road transport. The train fares are around one third of normal bus fares. In Colombo, about 15 to 20 per cent of the working population reach the city via the railways. A majority of these people are from other regional town centres and from suburban areas of Colombo city. Due to the lack of an efficient rail network covering Colombo city and its suburban areas, a majority of people rely on bus transport services. Recently, Colombo Metropolitan Regional Structure Plan (CMRSP) has prepared proposals for the construction of a circular rail network to cover Colombo city and its suburbs. If that proposal becomes operational, the passenger transport system may improve in Colombo.

3.4 Three-wheelers

Three-wheelers, which are imported mainly from India, are a recent addition (since the mid-1980s) to passenger transport and are used particularly for short trips in urban areas, as well as in rural areas of Sri Lanka. Three-wheelers are operated as individually-owned, hired vehicles with no control of operations—such as the number of vehicles permitted in certain locations, the fixing of meters for fares and the number of permitted passengers etc. The only regulatory factor is that registration is required with the Motor Traffic Department of Sri Lanka, with a license issued by the government annually and the need for annual insurance coverage of the vehicle. Three-wheeler services in the city have provided self-employment for many unemployed youths, as well as for those who have retired from their jobs. Many people who own three-wheelers rent them out to known operators on an agreed daily rent (for example, the person who rents a three-wheeler has to provide fuel and attend to minor repairs, and at the end of the day has to pay 200 to 300 Rupees to the owner). Therefore, the operation of three-wheelers has become a significant self-employment activity in the city.

According to the statistics of the Motor Traffic Department, there was a sharp increase in the registration of three-wheelers during the period 1992 to 2001 (i.e. from 15,252 in 1992 to 112,302 three wheelers in 2001).Although there is no reliable data on the number of three-wheelers operating within the city of Colombo, interviews with key interviewees revealed that around 50,000 three-wheelers are operated daily in the city as at 2002.

Most of the time, three-wheelers are used by passengers to reach to a destination in a relatively short period of time compared to the bus. In Colombo, three-wheelers are famous for emergency runs. The three-wheeler operators have themselves formed small associations based on the particular street or market place where they regularly operate.

Due to the non-regulated status of their service, three-wheeler operators used to exploit passengers by forcing them to pay high fares. Normally their minimum hiring charge is Rs.20 per km; however in the absence of a fare-meter, sometimes the passengers have to pay up to Rs.30 per km. During the night, as well as during rainy season, three-wheeler drivers charge unreasonable rates. Generally, three-wheeler operators are not recognized as respectable service providers. Since they started to be used by thugs, drug dealers and others who engage in social malpractices, three-wheeler drivers have lost their good reputation. Although they look for three-wheelers in the absence of other transport modes, passengers tend to see them as problem creators. This is primarily due to a lack of parking spaces for three-wheelers and the lack of fare control, as well as the violation of traffic rules and regulations by three-wheeler operators. Therefore, the operation of three-wheelers in the city is not regarded as a reliable transport mode for passengers, but as one that adds to the problems in the transport sector.

However, if the government can negotiate with the three-wheeler operators, their services can be well integrated into the city's public transport system. Although the above-mentioned deficiencies exist, three-wheelers currently provide an efficient service at places such as hospitals, markets, banks and near major employment centres of the city. Three-wheeler services are also available during off-peak hours, particularly during the night when private and public bus services are not available.

3.5 School vans and office staff transport

Along with the privatization of passenger transport services in Sri Lanka in the early 1980s, school vans and vans for office staff also began to enter into passenger transport services. School vans and office staff vans are operated by individuals, mostly on an owner-operated basis or operated by employing drivers.

Table 3.1. Total vehicle population in Sri Lanka (passenger vehicles only)

Class of vehicle	1992	%	1997	%	2001	%
CTB buses	13,927	1.76	14,083	1.24	16,546	1.16
Hiring buses and private buses	32,235	4.1	42,630	3.76	49,715	3.48
Dual purpose vehicles (vans)	38,909	4.91	99,407	8.82	141,496	9.98
Motor cars	17,225	22.0	202,451	18.0	241,399	16.88
Motor cycles	516,205	65.3	709,825	62.96	868,610	60.74
Three wheelers	15,252	1.93	59,119	5.24	112,302	7.85
Total	790,753	100.0	1,127,515	100.0	1,430,068	100.0

Source: Adopted from a statistical record of the Statistical unit of Department of Motor Traffic, Sri Lanka (2001)

Considering issues such as reliability, safety (the available government school buses are too crowded and sometimes school children used to travel hanging on to the foot-board, risking their lives) and many other factors, those people who can afford to pay send their children to school in school vans. School vans are small, having seating capacity of eight to 16 seats. The school vans and office staff transport vans are also unregulated, other than the requirement that they register with the Department of Motor Traffic and receive an annual license from the government, as well as the requirement that they obtain annual insurance coverage. The rates that the school vans charge are agreed with the users and the vans usually operate on the basis of a monthly fee, depending on the distance (usually for 20km of there and back trips per month per school child, the rate would be around 1,200 Rupees, which is approximately 20 times the cost of the monthly school season ticket on a CTB bus). For office staff for the same distance the rate would be around 1,500 Rupees per month, which is about four times the normal monthly bus fare per person. However, many people tend to use these passenger vans due to the inefficiency of the existing public passenger transport services in Colombo. For these hiring vans, there is always a defined group of users who pay an agreed monthly amount, as mentioned above.

The government has not introduced any regulations for the vans. However, it has been highlighted by many interviewees that allowing of a large number of passenger vans to enter to the city every day has further aggravated the city's traffic congestion. In common with the three-wheelers, there is no reliable data on the number of office and school vans entering to the city. However, key interviewees (particularly traffic police and municipal officials) estimated that there are about 10,000 to 12,000 school vans and staff transportation vans entering to the city daily. After unloading their passengers, over 90 per cent of such vans used to stay close to their passenger destinations (near schools and office complexes) until the passengers returned. However, due to a lack of proper parking for these vehicles, they used to encroach the pavements or would keep moving from place to place when they were chased by city traffic police.

3.6 Motorcycles

Motorcycles have become the cheapest and fastest transport mode for many people in urban as well as rural areas. Use of motorcycles began to increase particularly after 1988 with the liberalized economic policies that were introduced by the government at that time. Removal of import restrictions and various tax incentives contributed to the importation of motorcycles to Sri Lanka. According to the data available from the Department of Motor Traffic, the registered total number of motorcycles in the year 1992 was 516,205, a figure that rose to 709,825 in 1997 and 868,610 in 2001. Among the total passenger transport vehicles, motorcycles accounted for over 60 per cent in these years. Most of the working population in Colombo uses a motorcycle as the family vehicle, carrying two to four passengers (rider + three passengers). Due to the reckless and undisciplined driving of motorists, including private bus drivers, motorcyclists become frequent victims in road accidents (in the year 2000, 247 motorcyclists died in road accidents in the city of Colombo, out of a total of 2,140 accidental deaths). In this context, although people tend to use motorcycles as a convenient mode of transport for their daily travel, their vulnerability is always very high. One other important factor is that in Colombo and other parts of Sri Lanka, motorcycles are not used for hiring purposes. Motorcycles are used primarily for individual or family transportation needs alone.

In the case of low-income settlements, it was observed that motorcycles are very rarely used. Most people walk to the nearest bus route and use buses for their transport needs. When researchers inquired the reason, a majority of low-income people said it was too risky to use a motorcycle on the congested city roads and the use of public transport was cheap and less risky. Also, the use of three-wheelers as a family vehicle is more popular among low-income communities than motorcycles.

3.7 Motor cars

Motor cars are primarily used by middle-class and upper-income people, including those official cars that constitute a major part of the city traffic. Among the total passenger vehicle population, the percentage of motorcars varied between 22 per cent to 16.88 per cent during 1992 to 2001. However, in absolute numbers there has been a significant increase in motorcars, from 174,255 in 1992 to 241,399 in 2001.

The increase in the motorcar population may be partly attributed to the inefficiency in public transport, particularly the system's inability to cater to the demands of different category of people. Insufficient passenger load capacity on Sri Lanka Railway, as well as the poor public bus services, might have led people to resort to more individualistic modes of transport such as motorcars and motorcycles.

Increasing use of motorcars also contributes to increasing city traffic, particularly during peak hours of the day. Furthermore, lack of proper parking facilities within the city has compelled motorists to park their cars along the pavements and on street corners. Therefore, the government has to pay serious attention to regularizing the use of motorcars in its overall city traffic management plan in the future.

3.8 Pedal cycles

It is significant to note that the people living in the case study settlements, neither use motorcycles, nor pedal cycles to travel to their places of work or other destinations. (It was found that in each case study settlement, less than 10 people were using pedal or motorcycles). The reasons given by the people for not using the above modes of transport included those below.

i.   Being unable to afford a motor-cycle and the risk of being faced with accident when riding in the city.

ii.   The high risk involved in using a pedal cycle on the city roads of Colombo for two reasons. First is lack of a separate track for cyclists, while the second is the heavy traffic congestion on city roads. Therefore, people prefer to walk up to 1 kilometre from their homes to the nearest bus stop to catch a bus, or in certain cases in order to reach their place of work. Some of the adult women and school children indicated that they did not want to take the risk of walking along the pavements of city roads due to congestion and the potential risk of facing an accident, and therefore always prefer to take a bus, even for shorter distances. The lack of understanding of people's perspectives on their modes of travel by the authorities seems to have led to the abandonment of the cheap and environmentally friendly options of transport, such as pedal cycles, in Colombo.

Section 4

Analysis of the study findings

4.1 Introduction

For the purpose of this study, issues related to public transport have been identified based on the key themes. The themes are considered as those that emerged by the interaction between the user and the available service provisions of public transport and with respect to the key actors namely the users, service providers and regulators.

Under each theme, specific issues have been identified for convenient analysis of the research findings as detailed out in the Research Methodology. The identified key actors, themes and issues are indicated below.

4.2 Key actors, themes and issues

4.2.1 Key actors

The key actors involved in public transport provision and the use of transport services (as identified by the present study) are indicated below.

Users of public transport. One of the major user groups are people of urban poor settlements in the city of Colombo. First, the broader group includes people of the three major racial groups in the city i.e. Sinhalese, Tamils and Muslims. Secondly, different categories of persons, such as adult men, adult women, disabled people, elderly people, schoolgirls and schoolboys were included in order to cover the largest user groups.

In addition to the above, office workers and members of the general public who use public transport were interviewed. The details of these different categories are indicated in the following section of this report.

4.2.2 Service providers

The service providers included in the study are the public transport ownersand operators (drivers and conductors).

4.2.3 The regulators

The regulators included the authorities making policy and planning decisions, the regulators who issue permits and licenses, and those who regulate the operation of public transport (for example, the City Traffic Police and the Traffic Management Department of the Municipal Council). The last category included programme implementation institutions.

4.2.4 Key themes

Key themes that the users and providers raised, and issues relating to those key themes, are discussed in the following section of the report. This section only describes the key themes as identified by the key actors during the process of information gathering.

Table 4.1. Key actors and key themes

Key actors	Key themes
i. The users of pubic transport	• Pedestrian travel • Frequency and time of operation of public transport • Conditions of the transport mode/s • The service crew and their performance • Traveller information • Terminal facilities • Passenger rights • User satisfaction • Suggestions for service improvements
ii. Service providers	• Motivation behind investment made • Institutional support • Operational aspects of the service • Overall gains and satisfaction
Drivers and conductors	• Training / technical competency • Knowledge on the service • Facilities available • Job satisfaction • Suggestions for service improvements
iii. Regulators	• Policy and planning and planning provisions • Regulatory (conformity measurers) adopted • Regulatory (operational measures) • Programme implementations

The analysis of the research findings was carried out based on the above framework in order to better focus on the objectives of the study. A summary of interviews carried out is included under the section 4.3 summary statement.

4.3   Summary of interviews and meetings carried out

a.   Members of urban poor communities

Table 4.2. Interviewees from urban poor settlements

Name of urban poor settlements (case study)	Category of interviewees							Total
	Adult		Elderly / Physically handicapped		School		Com-munity leaders	
	Men	Women	Men	Women	Boys	Girls		
Poorwarama Settlement (relocated community)	05	05	03	03	04	04	02	26
259 Watta (shanty community)	05	05	03	03	04	04	02	26
Kadiranawatta (relocated community)	05	05	03	03	04	04	02	26
121 Watta (slum community)	05	05	03	03	04	04	02	26
Badowita Settlement (relocated community)	05	05	03	03	04	04	02	26
43 Watta, Bars Place	05	05	03	03	04	04	02	26
Total	30	30	18	18	24	24	12	156

b.   Passengers of public transport

Numbers

- Bus passengers   - 8 (3 men, 3 women)
- Rail passengers   - 8 (3 men, 3women)

c.   Public transport providers

- Bus owners   - 5
- Bus owners association's officials   - 2
- Bus conductors   - 6
- Bus drivers   - 6

d.   Para-transport providers

- Three-wheeler drivers   - 5
- Office vans   - 4
- School vans   - 4

e.   Representatives of regulatory agencies
(one responsible officer from each agency)

- Ministry of Transport
- Urban Development Authority
- Western Province Transport Authority
- National Transport Commission
- Sri Lanka Central Transport Board
- Colombo Municipal Council
- City Traffic Police

f.   R&D personnel (one from each category has been interviewed)

- Transport planners
- Urban sociologist
- Economist
- Research on public transport
- Women's Associations in urban poor settlements

g.   Research advisory meeting

Consisting of seven persons representing relevant organizations and three from Sevanatha meeting and reviewing the project activities. Their inputs at various stages of the project have been very significant.

h.   Focus group meetings

Two focus group meetings involving community members (men, women, children, youth and the elderly) were held in Poorwarama and Badowita settlements where viewpoints on access and the quality of public transport were discussed. The focus group meetings helped reinforce the findings of the user groups, while identifying new issues on related themes if any were proposed by the partnership.

4.4   Selection of case study settlements

Based on the scope of the research project, emphasis was put on including users of public transport from the urban poor communities in Colombo. For this purpose, identification of urban poor settlements became an important task. Considering the various factors influencing the existence of urban poor communities, criteria were developed for identifying appropriate settlements for the purposes of carrying out interviews with different user groups of public transport.

The criteria included those below.

i.   Type of settlements (i.e. in Colombo there are five major types of low-income settlements: slum settlements, non-upgraded squatter settlements, upgraded squatter settlements, upgraded slums, relocated settlements and low-cost floats). Of these, the upgraded squatter settlements, relocated settlements and upgraded slums form the majority of urban poor settlements. Therefore, communities belonging to these three categories were chosen.

ii. Geographical distribution within the city (in order to represent the main areas of concentration of urban poor settlements within the city).

iii. Size of the settlements (average household size, as well as some larger and some smaller).

iv. Distance to the nearest public transport route.

v.   Age of the settlement (consolidation factor / linkages with the city's development activities).

Based on the above criteria, already available data on urban poor communities in Colombo was used for identification of appropriate settlements.

Table 4.3. Distribution of urban poor settlements in Colombo City

Settlement type	No. of settlements	%	No. of housing units	%
Slums	1,071	71.1	25,500	38.6
Shanties (squatter settlements)	183	12.2	13,313	20.2
Low-cost flats	103	6.8	8,950	13.6
Relocated housing	97	6.4	14,814	22.4
Old deteriorated quarters	31	2.1	2,575	3.9
Unplanned permanent	21	1.4	870	1.3
Total	1,506	100	66,022	100

Source: Survey of Urban Low Income Settlements of Colombo, Sustainable Township Programme (STP) under the Ministry of Urban Development & Housing, 1997/98

The opinion of the municipal officials and members of research team, as well as the research advisory committee were sought in finally identifying the urban poor settlements for the research. The number of settlements thus identified was limited to six settlements. This number was agreed between the research team and the Research Coordinator of WEDC considering factors such as available time, resources, number of interviews to be completed and the depth of information to be collected for the purposes of the study.

The six settlements satisfying the above mentioned criteria were then called case study settlements where different categories of public transport users (i.e. the elderly and disabled, adult men, adult women and school children) were interviewed. A summary of selected settlements is indicated in the table below.

Table 4.4. Distribution of urban poor settlements in Colombo City

	Name & location of settlement	Type of settlement	Size of the settlement (household size)	No. of persons interviewed	Distance from the city centre (km)
1.	Kadirana Watta, Mattakkuliya, Colombo North	Relocated community	840	26	04
2.	Poorwarama Settlement, Colambage Mawatha, Colombo East	Relocated community	170	26	08
3.	259 Watta, Ferguson Road, Colombo North	Shanty community	123	26	03
4.	121 Watta, Maligawatta, Colombo 10	Slum settlement	102	26	03
5.	43 Watta, Barnes Place, Colombo 07	Slum community	56	26	05
6.	Badowita Settlement	Relocated community	1,141	26	08

Note: The word 'Watta' is used in local language to identify an urban low-income settlement

4.5 Profile of case study settlements

In order to familiarize itself with the identified case study settlements, the research team visited them and prepared a brief settlement profile of each prior to carrying out the survey. The information-gathering exercise for the settlement profile paved the way for developing a relationship with community leaders and members. The information exchange that took place during the carrying out of the interviews of identified community members was also passed to the community during the preparation of the settlement profile. Thus, the preparation of profile was a useful beginning to the study process. The completed settlement profiles are presented below.

Box 4.1. Profile of case study settlement — Kadirana Watta

1.0	Name and location of the settlement:		Kadirana Watta, Falm Road, Mattakkuliya.
1.1	Year of origin	:	1950
1.2	Type of the settlement	:	Relocated settlement
1.3	No. of households as of 2001	:	840
1.4	Municipal Ward	:	Colombo North
2.0	Land ownership of the settlement	:	Sri Lanka Land Reclamation and Development Corporation

2.1   Availability of basic infrastructure

➤	Water supply	:	Individual water connections
➤	Toilets	:	12 common toilets and 5 individual toilets connected to soak pits
➤	Access roads	:	20-foot-wide tarred road
➤	Stormwater drains	:	Open masonry drains
➤	Electricity	:	Available for individual houses

3.0	Availability of public transport to the settlement:	Not available
3.1	Distance to nearest public transport route:	½ kilometer
4.0	Type of employment of the majority of community:	Informal business activities and unskilled labourers
4.1	Distance to work place of the majority:	6 km

5.0   Distance to other services

- ➤ School   -   3 km
- ➤ Market   -   4 km
- ➤ Hospital   -   8 km
- ➤ Post office   -   ½ km

Box 4.2. Profile of case study settlement — Poorwarama Settlement

1.0	Name and location of the settlement:		Poorwarama Purawaraya, DC Colambage Mawatha, Kirulapone, Colombo 05
1.1	Year of origin	:	1998
1.2	Type of the settlement	:	Relocated settlement
1.3	No. of households as of 2001	:	170
2.0	Land ownership of the settlement	:	Road Development Authority
2.1	Availability of basic infrastructure		
	➤ Water supply	:	Individual connections
	➤ Toilets	:	2 common toilets (but majority have individual toilets); plans are underway for construction of a sewer scheme for the settlements
	➤ Access roads	:	15–20-foot-wide tarred road; all inner roads are gravel roads
	➤ Stormwater drains	:	None available
	➤ Electricity	:	Available for individual houses
3.0	Availability of public transport to the settlement:		None available
3.1	Distance to nearest public transport route:		½ kilometre
4.0	Type of employment of the majority of community:		Skilled and unskilled labourers, self-employment activities
4.1	Distance to workplaces of the majority:		5 to 6 km
5.0	Distance to other services		
	➤ School	-	½ km
	➤ Market	-	3 km
	➤ Hospital	-	4 km
	➤ Post office	-	½ km

Box 4.3. Profile of case study settlement — 259 Watta

1.0	Name and location of the settlement:		259 Watta, Ferguson Road, Colombo North
1.1	Year of origin	:	1971
1.2	Type of the settlement	:	Shanty settlement
1.3	No. of households as of 2001	:	123
2.0	Land ownership of the settlement	:	Private owner (original owner died and his representative used to collect rent from the occupants)

2.1 Availability of basic infrastructure

➤ Water supply	:	6 common taps; some houses have individual connections
➤ Toilets	:	6 male and 6 female common toilet units available
➤ Access roads	:	15-foot-wide tarred road
➤ Stormwater drains	:	None available
➤ Electricity	:	Available for individual connections

3.0	Availability of public transport to the settlement:		None available
3.1	Distance to nearest public transport route:		½ kilometre
4.0	Type of employment of the majority of community:		Unskilled labourers
4.1	Distance to workplace of the majority:		about 5 km

5.0 Distance to other services

➤ School	-	1 km
➤ Market	-	2 km
➤ Hospital	-	6 km
➤ Post office	-	½ km

Box 4.4. Profile of case study settlement — 121 Watta

1.0	Name and location of the settlement:		121 Watta, Maligawatta, Colombo 10
1.1	Year of origin	:	1960–1965
1.2	Type of the settlement	:	Slum settlement
1.3	No. of households as of 2001	:	102
2.0	Land ownership of the settlement	:	Private businessman who died about 20 years ago. Owner's relative collects rent from the houses.

2.1   Availability of basic infrastructure

➤ Water supply	:	Only one common tap
➤ Toilets	:	Individual toilets
➤ Access roads	:	22-foot-wide tarred road
➤ Wastewater & Storm	:	Open masonry drains water drains connected to a nearby canal
➤ Electricity	:	Available—individual house connections

3.0	Availability of public transport to the settlement:	None available
3.1	Distance to nearest public transport route:	¼ kilometre
4.0	Type of employment of the majority of community:	Informal business activities and unskilled labour work
4.1	Distance to workplaces of the majority:	about 3 to 4 km

5.0   Distance to other services

➤ School	-	¼ km
➤ Market	-	½ km
➤ Hospital	-	4 km
➤ Post office	-	200 m

Box 4.5. Profile of case study settlement — 43 Watta

1.0	Name and location of the settlement:		43 Watta, Barns Place, Kurunduwatta, Colombo 07
1.1	Year of origin	:	1959
1.2	Type of the settlement	:	Slum settlement
1.3	No. of households as of 2001	:	56
2.0	Land ownership of the settlement	:	Private (the original owner died and no one is collecting the rents at present)

2.1 Availability of basic infrastructure

	➤ Water supply	:	4 common taps and 4 individual taps
	➤ Toilets	:	4 common toilets and 3 individual toilets
	➤ Access roads	:	Gravel road
	➤ Stormwater drains	:	None available
	➤ Electricity	:	Available for individual houses

3.0	Availability of public transport to the settlement:	None available
3.1	Distance to nearest public transport route:	½ kilometre
4.0	Type of employment of the majority of community:	Informal businesses and daily labour work
4.1	Distance to workplaces of the majority:	3 to 4 km

5.0 Distance to other services

- ➤ School   -   1 km
- ➤ Market   -   1 km
- ➤ Hospital   -   1 km
- ➤ Post office   -   1 km

Box 4.6. Profile of case study settlement — Badowita Settlement

1.0	Name and location of the settlement:		Badowita, Attidiya, Ratmalana
1.1	Year of origin	:	1991
1.2	Type of the settlement	:	Relocated settlement
1.3	No. of households as per year 2001:		1,141
1.4	Municipal Ward	:	Attidiya North Municipal Ward of Dehiwala Mt. Lavinia Municipality
2.0	Land ownership of the settlement	:	Sri Lanka Land Reclamation and Development Corporation (SLLR&DC)

2.1 Availability of basic infrastructure

	➢ Water supply	:	Individual connections
	➢ Toilets	:	Individual toilets
	➢ Access roads	:	20–30-foot-wide tarred road
	➢ Stormwater drains	:	Available but not functioning properly
	➢ Electricity	:	Available for individual houses

3.0	Availability of public transport to the settlement:		Two private vans available but service is not regular
3.1	Distance to nearest public transport route:		2 to 3 km
4.0	Type of employment of the majority of community:		Men involved in informal business activities while women engage in housemaid work in nearby middle-income houses
4.1	Distance to workplace of the majority:		4 km

5.0 Distance to other services

	➢ School	-	3 km
	➢ Market	-	4 km
	➢ Hospital	-	6 km
	➢ Post office	-	½ km

4.6　Interviews of community members in case study settlements

Community members of the six selected case study settlements were interviewed in order to obtain their perspectives on the current status of public transport. The community members included;

i. **Senior citizens and disabled persons**. Senior citizens included both men and women above 65 years of age. Disabled persons were considered those who suffered from permanent disabilities and who needed the help of other people to move about. Under these two categories, 36 persons (18 men and 18 women) were interviewed.

ii. **Adult men**. Adult men included those above 25 years of age, married and living with a family. Thirty men were interviewed from the six case study settlements.

iii. **Adult women**. Adult women were those above 25 years, married with children. Thirty adult women were interviewed from the six case study settlements.

iv. **School children** (including both girls and boys above 10 years of age): Twenty-four schoolgirls and 24 schoolboys were interviewed from the six case study settlements.

v. **Community leaders**. Community leaders, both men and women, numbering 12 people were interviewed.

In addition to the members of urban poor settlements, bus and rail passengers, public transport providers, para-transport providers and representatives of regulatory agencies were interviewed. The key issues raised by these interviewees are summarized and presented below.

Section 5

Community perspectives of existing public transport

5.1 Senior citizens and disabled people

5.1.1 What senior citizens say about pedestrian travel

- We do not go out of the home except for an essential purpose because now the roads are too dangerous for us to walk. Even if we go out, we have to seek the help of our children or someone who is known to us.

- We walk along the pavements very carefully because we are scared of the reckless drivers, three-wheelers, potholes and uneven surfaces.

- Most of the time we use the yellow coloured pedestrian crossings to cross to the other side of the road, but even on the pedestrian crossings, drivers, motorcyclists and three-wheeler drivers do not slow down their vehicles.

- We have to wait for a long time until the road becomes clear and the drivers slow down their vehicles so that we can cross the road.

- Indiscriminate stopping of buses to take passengers onboard is a real nuisance for us while walking, as the buses almost run us down unexpectedly.

- Most of the roads are too narrow for the vehicles and sometimes vehicles run over the pavements when they overtake another vehicle.

- Hawkers encroach upon pavements, and the boutiques and shops have extended their businesses onto the pavements.

- Cars, vans and three-wheelers park on the pavement and so we have to walk on the road, which is really dangerous.

- I travel about by my wheelchair. I am very careful and keep to my side of the road, but private bus drivers blow the horn to push me aside.

5.1.2 What senior citizens say about bus shelters

- We can't stand and wait for a long time for a bus so we need a place to sit. But there are no proper bus shelters. The available bus shelters are not properly maintained. Nor do they have roofs and seats.

- Bus shelters are often occupied by beggars and drug addicts, and are made dirty.

- Bus shelters do not provide any traveller information.

- They seem not to be maintained by anyone.

5.1.3   What senior citizens say about the behaviour of bus drivers

- Private bus drivers often do not take us when they see us at the bus stop; they halt the bus a little away from the stop, either in front or behind. They treat us as a nuisance. We feel very embarrassed.

- They do not stop buses for the school children either.

- We have to wait at the bus stop for CTB buses. They do not come very frequently.

- Private bus drivers do not give us enough time to get in or get out of the bus, even if we do have a chance to get in.

- Sometimes private bus drivers do not stop at the right bus stop for us to get off. They take us further up, sometimes one bus stop or more, and when we protest they ask us why we have not come near to the door to get off.

- They drive very fast and apply the brakes suddenly without thinking of the passengers. If we did not get a seat, it is difficult for us to keep standing inside the bus.

- Some drivers are drunk.

- I seriously doubt whether some of these private bus drivers are capable of driving such heavy vehicles. I do not know whether they have licences or enough experience.

- The private bus drivers gather at the bus stops or drive very slow to get more passengers. The moment they see the next bus coming behind, they start racing.

- We have quite often seen that they simply disregard traffic rules and regulations. They pass traffic lights even when the red light is on.

- CTB bus drivers are better than private bus drivers. But sometimes they too do not give us enough time to get out of the bus.

- Although smoking is prohibited inside the bus and signs are displayed, some drivers smoke while driving.

5.1.4   What senior citizens say about the behaviour of bus conductors

- Private bus conductors keep shouting at passengers to move forward or to go back, even though the buses are already crowded.

- They cheat and do not give our balance (change). When we ask for it, they scold us.

- Sometimes the private bus conductors delay giving change and when we are about to get off, they give us the change in small coins. There is no time for us to count the money, we get down and often find that they have cheated us.

- They do not issue tickets; forgetting that we have paid they keep asking for money. When we say that we have paid, they do not believe us and use rough and filthy words.

- Private bus conductors encourage the drivers to stop anywhere on the road to take passengers onboard.

- Some bus conductors pull the bell to signal the driver to drive off even before we get off. I once fell down and got injured.

- When we ask for the bus route, some private bus conductors tell lies to avoid us and say that their bus does not take the route we wish to travel.

- When we argue, the private bus conductors have one definite answer! They say, 'If you have any problem, get out and take another bus. We have enough people to take.' On such occasions, most of the time other passengers keep quiet, without supporting us.

- I have witnessed that some private bus conductors harass women and girls. They touch women and ladies when they get onto or off the bus, and they creep in between aisle of the crowded bus, pressing against women.

- The private bus conductors keep silent even when they know that pickpockets have got in.

5.1.5 What senior citizens say about the facilities available inside the buses

It was observed that most of the senior citizens preferred to use CTB buses for their journeys rather than private buses. Therefore, their views on CTB buses are listed below.

- CTB buses are more spacious and usually less congested.

- The CTB bus conductors do not cheat us and they issue tickets for the journey.

- In CTB buses, some seats are allocated for clergy, pregnant women and disabled people, but not for the elderly. However, when we get into a bus, the conductor usually helps us find a seat.

- We can easily identify CTB buses as they are painted with a colour and have the CTB emblem.

- We remember when there were double-deckers running in Colombo, normally they were less crowded. Those days we did not have problems travelling by bus.

- We can identify buses looking at their destination board and route number.

- On CTB buses, passengers usually offer their seats to elderly people.

- CTB buses generally do not go race or travel too fast.

- Some years ago there were inspectors who checked tickets on CTB passengers but we do not find them now.

- We rely on CTB buses because they are government buses. They are large in size and usually we can get seats.

- 'I consider playing cassette recorders inside buses a good thing because the drivers will not fall asleep' (BD/ELRD/FMS/58/1/3).

Prior to the 1960s, CTB buses were allocated on the **basis** of people's demands. But at present it has become a political activity.

5.1.6 Suggestions made by senior citizens to improve public transport services

On pedestrian travel

- Pavements should not be blocked; they need to be spacious and well maintained, considering the very large numbers of pedestrians who use these common spaces.

- Pedestrians, too, should be well-informed so that they use pavements only to walk and use yellow pedestrian crossings to cross the roads. If not, they should be fined.

Box 5.1. The story of Mr. Pushpakumara, a disabled person in Poorwarama Community—'*No hope of moving about fearlessly*'

Mr. Pushpakumara is a 29-year-old disabled person who lives in the Poorwarama community. Both his legs are non-functional and he uses a wheelchair for all his daily movements within the settlement and around about. But for longer distances he depends on relatives to accompany him. According to his experience, there is no consideration for disabled people like him in the preparation of designs and the operation of public transport. The disabled are being neglected by society. There are no designated seats or spaces for disabled people inside a bus. But, sometimes, people offer their seat to him voluntarily; however, this is not happening at peak hours. It is so dangerous getting in and getting off the bus, even with a helper, due to the impatience of bus crews. Most of the time, the conductor rings the bell before he is able to get in or off the bus. One day, the driver drove off before he was able to get off and he fell down from the bus and was badly injured. The conductor and all passengers blamed him, because they were becoming late.

Besides travelling on buses, he cannot use his wheelchair to move along any of the city streets because the pavements are so narrow and the surface is uneven. There is no place on the pavement to take in his wheelchair. Therefore, he has to run his wheelchair by the side of the pavement, which is very dangerous. because motorists have encroached the pavement side of the road and sometimes reckless drivers do not give him room to use his wheelchair. Therefore, it is a real frustration and a risk for people like him to go out of their homes to the street. He feels they are being discriminated against, knowingly or unknowingly, by the present arrangements and planning of public transport in the country. He feels really sorry for himself and the people who are responsible for managing the transport service.

Bus shelters

- Bus stops should be provided with bus shelters. They should include seats, roof covers and traveller information. Also they need to be well maintained.

Bus drivers and conductors

- There should be a system to catch those drivers who speed and they should be fined.

- Continuous training programmes for drivers and conductors are necessary to make them aware of traffic rules and regulations, as well as how to treat passengers.

- They need to be made aware that they are providing a service for which passengers are paying.

- Driving licenses should be checked regularly as some drivers may have bogus licenses.

- A set of standards should be introduced for recruiting private bus conductors, such as education levels, a minimum age, number of years experience etc. The government or relevant agencies should intervene in this matter.

- TV advertisements should be introduced to make drivers and conductors and passengers aware that senior citizens and persons with physical handicaps need to be treated equally, in the same manner as other passengers.

- The issuing of tickets should be made compulsory.

- When an issue arises inside a bus concerning a particular passenger, others too should intervene and stand up for their common rights. This means there should be programmes to create and enhance passenger rights.

Facilities inside the buses

- The existing roof bells should be removed, because they are too high. Easily visible bells at arm's length should be fixed (or preferably pull-type bells should be provided).

- One or two seats should be allocated for elderly people. They should be located at the rear of the bus.

- Spacious hood racks must be provided for keeping passengers' bags.

- Elderly people should be allowed to get onto and off the bus slowly and carefully.

Regulating public transport

- Government must regularly obtain the views of general public on the status of public transport facilities.

- Drivers and conductors must be made aware of their responsibility to ensure the safety of passengers, and must respect passengers' rights.

- Buses should be operated according to a proper timetable.

- The bus boards should be in all three languages (Sinhala, Tamil and English) and must be large enough to be seen from a distance.

- Buses should be stopped only at specified bus stops.

- Buses should be prevented from congregating and congesting certain places.

- A notice must be displayed inside buses indicating when and how passengers can make complaints against any injustice they face during their bus journey.

5.2   Adult women

5.2.1   What adult women say about pedestrian travel

- Pedestrian travel is a real problem for us because the three-wheeler drivers and young boys make offensive jokes. Sometimes they purposely turn their vehicles towards us to get our attention.

- We used to walk on the right hand side of the road and cross the road only at pedestrian crossing. However, motorists do not care about us, even when we use the yellow crossings.

- Normally we have to wait at the pedestrian crossing for five to ten minutes until the road is clear to cross over to the other side.

- Most of the three-wheelers are parked on the pavement or by the side of the pavements blocking the way for pedestrians.

- Some three-wheeler drivers make filthy jokes and we have to avoid them.

- Sometimes not only three-wheeler drivers, but also some passengers address filthy words at us when we walk along the pavement.

- During peak hours (mornings from 7.00 to 9.00 a.m. and evenings from 4.30 to 7.00 p.m.) it is very difficult to cross the city roads. When we step onto pedestrian crossings some motorists scold us. They do not care for pedestrians.

- Most of the pavements are encroached upon by businessmen, vendors and parked vehicles. Therefore, we cannot use the pavements. We cannot walk with our children either, because the pavements are too narrow and crowded.

- It is dangerous for women to walk at night along the inner access roads to the settlement. Thieves snatch our bags and jewellery. They also harass young girls. Sometimes men attempt to rape girls.

- Thieves normally break the streetlights to make the road dark at night.

- During the rainy season, it is difficult to use the access roads in our settlement. Roads become water logged and full of muddy holes.

Box 5.2. Story of Ms. Salgadu, Badowita Urban Poor Settlement— *She tells us about a community that is dissatisfied due to the lack of reliable public transport services*

Ms. Salgadu is a forty-four years old community activist in Badowita relocated settlement. Before her family came to this community, they were living in a shanty community located on a canal bank reservation near the Pamankada area in Colombo city. This location provided easy access for their daily travel. It was only walking distance for her children's school and to the bus stand. However, all members of her community were relocated to the Badowita by the government under its Canal Rehabilitation Project. At the beginning, there were no proper access roads to the community. They had to walk one and a half kilometers daily to the nearest bus stop.

'It was very difficult to walk on our access roads on rainy days due to the poor road conditions and floods. Our community made several requests to the relevant officials for them to improve this situation, but nothing has happened. Therefore, we discussed this problem at our community meetings. One community member who had saved some money from his job overseas agreed to purchase a small van to provide transport. There was a big celebration on the first day we had the van service for the Badowita community. However, it functioned for just two months because the owner did not show interest in continuing the service due to the bad road conditions and heavy running costs.' Subsequently, the community invited the Minster of Highways and Transport to participate in one of their meetings during the election period.

The Minister realized the poor condition of the access roads and he promised to improve the main community access road and to provide a CTB bus especially for the Badowita community. As a result, the community of Badowita received one CTB bus for their travel. It functioned according to a timetable and made two trips per day at 7.30 a.m from the community to the city and 2.30 p.m from the city to the community. However, the service was not adequate for the more than 1,000 families who live in the community. Therefore, there was a huge queue for the bus during these times. Gradually, a few community members invested their savings intovehicles for transport in the community. Now, the community has two private vans and about ten three-wheelers, which are owned by the community members. However, with this competition the CTB bus was withdrawn from Badowita. People now have to depend on the private transport operators. They are not punctual or reliable. Also, community members have to spend more on transport. This is an unnecessary expense when compared to their early location. Since the Badowita settlement is located a long distance from all services (markets, schools, hospitals, post offices and the urban local authority), people find it extremely difficult to visit these places due to the inadequate transport facilities. The private vans do not operate to a fixed schedule; they wait for hours for a full load of passengers. Therefore, I think most of the community members walk about one and a half kilometres distance to the public bus route, said Ms. Salgadu.

5.2.2   What adult women say about bus shelters

- There are no properly covered bus shelters. Therefore, we face many problems such as:
    - difficulty in sheltering from the rain and sun;
    - passengers not being able to identify the bus stop;
    - bus drivers stopping their buses any place they wish; and
    - the available spaces for bus stops are encroached upon by three-wheelers.

- Some bus stops are used by drug addicts, beggars and prostitutes, especially at night. Therefore, women do not usually wait at such bus stops.

5.2.3   What adult women say about the regulatory aspects of public transport

- Passengers do not know where to complain when they have faced a problem while travelling on a bus.

- There is no passenger association or any other known civil society organization where passengers can make a complaint.

- We do not have faith in the police either because we believe the police take bribes from the bus crews and do not listen to passengers.

5.2.4   What adult women say about behaviour of bus drivers and conductors

Behaviour of conductors especially (private bus conductors)

- They always shout at us ordering us to move backward and forward.

- The conductors do not talk politely to passengers. They scold passengers if any passenger raises an issue.

- The conductors help only when we get onto the bus; when we get down from the bus they shout at us to get off quickly. Sometimes they signal the driver to drive off before we have got off.

- Normally, private bus conductors do not issue tickets. When we ask for a ticket they say not to worry and move forward, that they will issue the ticket later.

- When conductors realize that a ticket inspector is going to get onto the bus, they quickly issue tickets to passengers that do not correspond with the trips that the passengers are making.

- Private bus conductors purposefully delay returning the balance money (change) to passengers. Usually, we forget to ask them for our change.

- There is no limit to the number of passengers a bus can take, particularly with private buses. Often in private buses, the conductors keep taking on passengers, disregarding the inconvenience and discomfort caused.

- Conductors often touch women and young girls unnecessarily when they get onto the bus.

- When they see an old person, a disabled person or even a member of the clergy waiting for a bus, the private bus conductors signal the driver either not to stop at that point or to stop some distance away from that particular passenger.

- Sometimes private bus conductors become involved in conflicts with other bus drivers and conductors. They exchange filthy words, disregarding the passengers.

Behaviour of conductors (CTB buses)

- Conductors on CTB buses are not so bad as private bus conductors.
- Sometimes the CTB conductors too do not issue tickets, particularly for short trips.
- They do not normally cheat passengers and return their change.
- CTB conductors do not shout at passengers unreasonably inside the bus.
- They also help those passengers who need help such as the elderly, disabled and children, when they are getting onto or getting off the bus.

5.2.5 What adult women say about the drivers of private buses

- Private bus drivers often race with other buses on the road, risking the lives of passengers.
- Most of the time when passengers want to get off at a particular bus stop they do not halt at the bus stop; instead they stop the bus where they can pick up another passenger.
- Private bus drivers congregate at junctions, which is a real nuisance for passengers.
- Also, some drivers shout at passengers asking them to move forwards or backwards in the bus when they do not have a seat.
- Some drivers blow the horn unnecessarily, irritating the passengers.
- We often come across drunken drivers who drive recklessly, risking our lives.
- The private bus drivers are not polite. They always blame the passenger if a passenger raises an issue.

5.2.6 What adult women say about the facilities available inside the buses

- We like travelling in CTB buses. They are less crowded.
- Sometimes we like the playing of cassette recorders inside the buses. Passengers can enjoy music and nice songs.
- In private buses there are no seats allocated for the disabled, clergy or pregnant women. Therefore, such passengers have to wait until someone offers them a seat.
- The route number and the name of the destination (bus board) are not large enough to read from a distance.
- The name of the destination is written in Sinhala only, when it should be in all three languages.
- Some private buses use similar exterior colours to the CTB buses, therefore we cannot identify them. Regular CTB passengers get confused and face difficulties (especially monthly season ticket holders and school children).
- The interiors of most private buses and CTB buses are very poor. The seats are torn, the side mirrors are broken and the interiors are not cleaned.
- Some private buses are small coaches, which have low roof levels, narrow spaces between the seats and no spaces to keep luggage

5.2.7 Suggestions to improve the access and quality of public transport

Facilities inside the bus

- The handrails of all the buses are too high; it is very difficult for women to hold the handrails. They should be fixed at a lower level for the convenience of passengers.

- The roof bells are also too high to use. They should be fixed close to the seats and should be visible.

- The bus operators should not be allowed to pack too many passengers inside the buses. They should be regulated to take passengers on the basis of the seating capacity (passenger overcrowding should be controlled).

- The bus crew and other passengers should be educated to respect women passengers. There should be mass awareness programmes to educate people on this issue.

- Passengers should be educated not to smoke inside the bus, as well as not to throw trash.

Regulating the public transport

- Women have no information about how to take action against the harassment they face as passengers. Therefore, there should be programmes to raise awareness on their rights and where to make complaints / suggestions.

Pedestrian travel

- Most of the pavements are encroached upon by vendors and motorists, therefore, pedestrians have no space on the pavements. The pavements should be wide enough and cleared for pedestrians.

- Pedestrians are used to crossing busy roads from wherever they like, which should be regulated by providing designated pedestrian crossings and road barriers.

- The pavements should be properly planned and constructed to ensure convenient travel, especially for women, children and elderly persons.

- Other facilities, such as wastebins, benches along the pavement, shady trees etc. should be provided to encourage pedestrians to walk along the city's streets.

Drivers and conductors

- There must be a proper procedure and minimum qualifications for bus drivers and conductors.

- The jobs of bus driver and conductor must be recognized and promoted as a profession.

- There must be regular training programmes for drivers and conductors on traffic rules, regulations, the rights of passengers and how to treat passengers.

Bus shelters

- Bus shelters should be properly planned and constructed to provide adequate protection for passengers from the sun and rain.

- At central junctions, there should be facilities in bus shelters for the passengers to form queues to ensure women and children are not discriminated against when they are getting onto the buses.

5.3   Adult men

5.3.1   What adult men say about pedestrian travel

- During peak hours (7.00 to 9.00 a.m. and 4.00 to 6.00 p.m.) pedestrians cannot walk along pavements because they are encroached upon by vendors.

- Normally, most passengers do not care about traffic regulations. They ignore traffic signs and try to cross the road ignoring pedestrian crossings.

- Most of the low-income community members are likely to use pedal cycles to go to work, but there is no designated space for pedal cycles on the roads. Therefore, it is dangerous to use bicycles.

- Some pedestrian crossings are not provided at the proper locations. Therefore, passengers cross the road from places that are convenient to them.

- Heavy vehicle congestion has resulted in pollution of city roads with smoke and dust. Also, due to the dangerous driving of motorists, pedestrians do not feel like walking freely along street.

5.3.2   What adult men say about the regulatory aspects of public transport

- Passengers have witnessed that a majority of drivers and conductors do not respect traffic rules and regulations.

- It was observed that inspectors usually check the bus documents, i.e. route permit etc., but the bus condition is not inspected by anyone i.e. tyres, signal lights, the interior condition, cleanliness and the exterior condition. Because of this situation, buses are not fit for passenger transport, and are operated on streets risking people's lives.

- Most of the buses do not operate to a fixed timetable. Some buses congregate at junctions for about 10 to 20 minutes, wasting the valuable time of passengers. When passengers complain at such occasions, the conductor and the driver blame the passengers.

- Information is not available to passengers as to where to make a complaint about any injustice they face during their bus journey.

- Passengers are aware that there are several government organizations responsible for managing public transport. But they have doubts about whether these organizations perform the duties entrusted to them. There is no relationship between these organizations and passengers.

5.3.3   What adult men say about the bus shelters

- Because there were no specific bus shelters, passengers get onto the buses from anywhere on the road. The bus drivers also stop anywhere, which results in traffic congestion and inconvenience to passengers.

5.3.4   Facilities inside the bus

- In most of the buses, there is no bell available. Passengers have to shout when they want to get off the bus. On certain buses the bell is not convenient. People cannot find or reach the bell.

5.3.5 What adult men say about conductors and drivers

- Private bus conductors often fail to return the balance of money (change). They keep postponing when asked for the change.

- Few private bus conductors are regular employees; nor are they trained. Therefore, they seem to work in an irresponsible manner; their only objective is to make their day's earnings.

- Sometimes we come across private conductors and drivers who are drunk. They scold passengers and drive the buses recklessly.

- Most private bus conductors and drivers behave like thugs. Therefore, when the passengers or police take action against them, they go on strike. They operate on a monopoly basis. Passengers do not have such an influential position.

5.3.6 Suggestions to improve the access and quality of public transport
Pedestrian travel

- There should be some control on the volume of traffic during peak hours in the mornings and evenings. Heavy vehicles, such as container carriers and trucks, should not be allowed to travel during peak hours on city roads.

- Most of the pavements are encroached upon by businessmen and motorists. Pavements should be clear and provided for pedestrians.

- Colour lights should be installed at pedestrian crossings in order to ensure the safety of pedestrians.

- Notices should be displayed along pavements, as well as at important places such as pedestrian crossings, providing pedestrian information.

- The Road Development Authority must take quick action to repair the roads when they are broken /dug by the Water or Telecom Authority for their service lines.

- Unnecessary billboards and displays should not be allowed on the streets because they are a nuisance for pedestrians.

- Most pavements are too narrow. Pedestrians cannot use them safely. Therefore, pavements should be constructed to reasonable standards where pedestrians, especially women and children, can walk safely.

- 'Roads should be kept clean and traffic should be controlled properly, like what we see on TV in other countries' (KDR/ADULT/ ML/43/S/4/6).

- Pedestrians cross the roads wherever they think it is appropriate. This should be regulated. In the city streets people should be allowed to cross roads only at designated pedestrian crossings.

Bus shelters

- The existing bus shelters are too small and are poorly maintained. They should be provided with space sufficient for at least 10 to 15 people. They should have a strong roof to cover one or two seats for elderly people and pregnant women.

- Most of the existing bus shelters are dirty. People throw rubbish around the bus shelter. Therefore, they must be provided with rubbish bins.

- Due to the lack of proper bus shelters, passengers wait all over the street and stop the buses, which is a real nuisance. This also contributes to traffic congestion.

- Bus shelters should not be covered at the sides because beggars, prostitutes and drug addicts occupy such bus shelters.

- 'They should be provided with information relating to passenger transport, the buses that stop at that particular shelter, the timetable and other passenger information. Bus shelters should not be used only for communal advertisements' (PR/ADLT/ML/S/33/1/8).

Regulating pubic transport

- Private bus drivers must be trained to observe traffic rules and regulations.

- Drivers must be made to pay large fines if they break traffic rules and engage in reckless driving.

- Pedestrians must also be charged when they break traffic regulations.

- Inspectors must be employed to carry out regular checks on private and CTB buses in order control the breaking of traffic rules and regulations.

- There must be strict procedures to ensure the mechanical fitness of the buses before permitting them to operate on the roads.

- 'We understand that there are many rules and regulations for the control of public transport in the country, but we are worried that the authorities do not implement those rules' (KDR/ADLT/ML/T/20/3-6).

- Most private bus conductors do not issue tickets to passengers. This problem should be regulated.

- Private bus drivers speed and drive recklessly, risking the lives of passengers. High-speed driving should be controlled.

Box 5.3. Story of Nimesha, a schoolgirl in Kadirana Community—
'A girl who wishes to travel on a school bus but no luck'

Nimesha is a 15-year-old schoolgirl from Kadirana community. She uses public transport to go to her school, which is 5 kilometres away from her community. There is a small school very close to her community, but her parents believe that this school does not have good facilities and teachers. Therefore, they send Nimesha to a school in the city. According to Nimasha's experiences travelling on public buses, she finds it is very difficult to get onto the buses during school hours because conductors consider the school children a problem. They do not stop the buses for school children because most of them are half-fare ticket users.

'I find it is difficult to carry my school bag inside the bus during my journey, because there is no space for the bag. Normally, I do not get a seat either in the morning or on my return after school. My friends and I, all of us, travel standing on the bus. We also prefer travelling standing when the bus is not crowded. When it is heavily crowded we always get crushed between people. My clothes get dirty. One day I lost my water bottle inside the bus. I think someone must have stolen it during the rush. I feel tired after travelling on the bus. I wish we had a good school bus and could travel freely.'

- In the meantime, certain buses congregate at central junctions wasting the time of passengers. There should be a definite time schedule and speed limits for passenger buses.

- 'I understand that the government is not paying sufficient attention to private bus operation, school vans, three-wheelers and other hiring vans etc. that transport passengers. Therefore, passengers suffer a lot. This situation must be rectified' (KDR/ADLT/ML/43/S/14/6).

- Most of the buses that operate in and around Colombo do not operate to a timetable. Therefore, especially in the evenings and at night there are no buses on street. People have to hire three-wheelers and / or vans, paying large sums of money to meet their transport needs. Therefore, proper management of existing buses should be considered as a priority of the government.

- The city traffic police must employ more policemen, particularly at junctions and market places during peak hours to control the traffic. Where there are no traffic police, private bus drivers in particular drive their buses completely on wrong side of the road.

5.4   School children

5.4.1   What school children say about the bus shelters

- The existing bus stops are not clean. They are not properly maintained. They are made dirty by displaying various posters.

- When we get onto the bus, especially in the morning, adults do not care about us. They push us aside and rush to the buses. There is no organized queue at the bus stop for people to get onto the buses.

- School children do not like to throw wastepaper and wrappings on the road or at the bus stops, but since there are no waste bins provided we throw them on the road.

5.4.2   What school children say about regulatory aspect of buses

- School children are harassed by other passengers in the bus (physical harassment). They feel there is no place to make complaints and hence feel compelled to tolerate the harassment and keep quiet.

- Most school children are not aware of their rights as passengers of public transport. Therefore, they feel they should be made aware of their rights and responsibilities.

- School buses are only available for some recognized schools in the city. The children of poor settlements who attend less prominent schools do not have a school bus service. Therefore, they have to use ordinary passenger buses, which is difficult, but there is no alternative.

5.4.3   What school children say about pedestrian travel

- When school children cross the road using pedestrian crossings, drivers do not normally give way to children.

- Some pedestrian walkways are not properly constructed and children sometimes fall and get hurt.

- 'Most of the pavements are narrow, hence I cannot catch hold of my mother's arm and walk with her together along the pavement,' says one schoolboy.

- On rainy days our uniforms get dirty because of splashes of muddy water from fast moving vehicles.

- Road names are not properly displayed on the streets and we sometimes get lost as a result. Proper name boards on roads are necessary.

- Most three-wheeler drivers harass schoolgirls. They also make filthy remarks and suggest bad things.

- Sometimes we cannot walk along the pavements due to the thick vehicle smoke. Our clothes get dirty and we also find it difficult to breath.

5.4.4 What school children say about bus conductors and drivers

- Some bus conductors and drivers wear dirty clothes. They appear to be very dirty people. When a conductor wears dirty clothes and passes by, our clothes also get dirty. We would prefer them to wear clean clothes, preferably a uniform.

- Sometime conductors do not like us occupying a seat. They ask us to travel standing.

- The conductors often do not like us carrying our school bags. They shout at us to keep the bag outside the bus.

- They never help us to get inside the buses.

- When we (girls) give money to conductors they keep pressing our fingers. When we complain about such incidences, they usually scold us on some other issue.

- When bus drivers speed and race one another, and when they suddenly apply the brakes, we get thrown about since we cannot hold the handrail because it is too high.

- The private bus conductors always cheat us. They do not return our change to us.

- Bus drivers sometimes fail to stop the bus at the bus stop; instead they take us further from the bus stop, which is an inconvenient to us.

5.4.5 What school children say about the facilities inside the buses

- School children cannot see the name board of the buses clearly.

- The handrail is too high to hold. Therefore, we have to hold onto the seat edges while we are standing.

- There is no space for us to keep our school bags.

- We schoolgirls do not like to sit on dirty seats because our dresses get dirty.

- The bell is fixed onto the roof, which is too high for us to push.

5.4.6 School children's suggestions

Pedestrian travel

- There should be signal lights at yellow pedestrian crossings to ensure safe road crossing by school children.

- A clear section of the pavement should be designated for pedestrian travel; vendors and motorists should not be allowed to encroach upon this section.

Bus shelters

- Buses should stop at bus stops only. Otherwise school children will have to walk or run to catch a bus, which is always dangerous for children.

Bus drivers and conductors

- There must be minimum qualifications and training for drivers and conductors.

- Bus drivers and conductors must be forced to wear uniforms.

- The conductors must be instructed to issue tickets to passengers.

Facilities inside the buses

- Facilities, such as the seats, racks and the bell inside the bus, should be designed and fixed for convenient use by children.

- The insides of the buses should display information and messages that are of interest to children (at least these can be provided in school buses).

- The doors of the buses must be able to close to protect children from falling off the bus.

Regulating the public transport

- Using mass media, awareness programmes should be launched by the government focussing on 'how to safeguard children's rights on the road'.

- More school buses should be provided in the morning and at the end of the school day to ensure convenient transport facilities for school children.

- Bus name boards should be large enough to read from a reasonable distance and should be visible to children.

- Queues should be formed at the bus stops so that children can get equal access to buses.

- There must be regulatory limitations to prevent overloading of passengers.

- There must be rules to insist that tickets must be issued to passengers. School children are usually blamed and are cheated by conductors as a result of the non-issue of tickets.

5.5 Office workers who use public transport (buses)

5.5.1 What office workers say about the facilities at bus stops

- There are no facilities, such as telephone booths near bus stops.

- Existing bus stops are not properly maintained. Therefore, passengers stand anywhere that is convenient for them to get onto a bus.

5.5.2 Rules and regulations

- During peak hours, most of the buses are crowded so some passengers travel on the steps.

- Passengers do not know to whom they should complain when there is a problem relating to their travel.

61

> **Box 5.4. Story of Ms. Sunethra, a young working women in 259 Watta community—One of the *silent worriers who use public transport***
>
> Ms. Sunethra is a 23 years old lady who lives in 259 Watta community. She works in a Garment Factory, which is located about 20 km away from her residence. Everyday she has to travel standing on the bus; there is a space only for one foot. Because of the rush to get into the bus, there is a lot of pushing and shouting and the passengers end up getting into quarrels with each other. The conductors do not care about the passengers' safety, they keep on loading people in their greed for money. They always shout at us to get on quickly, so as to not waste the time of the other passengers. But at certain places the bus keeps lagging for ten to fifteen minutes. In some buses there is a seat allocated for pregnant women. But, most of the time men occupy this seat. As a working woman, it is necessary to wear decent, nice looking clothes. But, men pass indirect remarks and try to make jokes at us. Most of the conductors ask for the bus fare from women by tapping them on their shoulders. But there are notices inside the buses saying not to harass women passengers. I think because the information is not widely known to people, and also because passengers do not know to whom to complain, the women face many problems inside the buses. Due to a lack of passengers' voices, women become the frequent victims among bus passengers, said Sunetra.

5.5.3 What office workers say about pedestrian travel

- There is traffic congestion during peak hours due to the uncontrolled traffic movement (i.e. allowing container carriers, lorries, trucks etc. along with passenger transport), which delays their journey to the office.

- It was observed that passengers and motorist blatantly violate traffic rules and regulations.

- Due to lack of proper vehicle parking facilities in the city, motorists park on the pavements and roadside, which is an inconvenience to pedestrians.

- Sometimes garbage is dumped on the pavement, which is an inconvenience to pedestrians.

5.5.4 What office workers say about the behaviour of drivers and conductors

- Conductors do not respect passengers. They do not issue tickets. Private bus conductors usually keep taking on passengers. They often cheat passengers by not handing over the change.

- Private bus drivers speed and race with other buses. They keep blowing the horn unnecessarily.

- The crew members do not wear uniforms. Most of the private bus conductors wear dirty clothes.

5.5.5 Facilities inside the buses

- In most buses, interior conditions are very poor. The seats are dirty, rusty and the floors are not cleaned.

- Usually, the insides of buses are noisy due to the shouting of conductors as well as the playing of cassettes.

- The broken shutters make unpleasant noises inside the buses.

5.6   Railway passengers

5.6.1   What they say about terminal facilities

• In small stations there is no visible name board to provide information.

• There are no adequate toilet facilities in the station (Kirulapone)

• The railway workers stage frequent strikes causing severe inconvenience to passengers.

• The announcements of train movements at most of the stations are not clear. The passengers cannot hear the announcements properly.

• The train timetables are not always reliable. Delays and train cancellations are regular events faced by passengers.

• Women are usually harassed at stations, particularly during the night.

• In most of the suburban stations, platforms are not properly constructed. Therefore, children and women find it difficult to get on and off the train.

• Women are harassed when they are on the trains. Sometimes a woman is offered a seat by a man, but when he stands he stares at the women.

5.7   Perspectives of private bus conductors relating to their jobs

Representing different parts of the city, five conductors were interviewed. They were all between age 26 and 31. Except for one person, none of the others had reached secondary level education. Four out of the five were unmarried. The views expressed by these conductors on their employment and their knowledge of the legal aspects of the job, along with the difficulties they faced and their suggestions for providing an improved public transport service, were very interesting.

5.7.1   The reason for selecting the job

• Since there is difficulty finding a job with their qualifications, they have chosen the job of a bus conductor.

• All that was required was some contact with the bus drivers to find this job.

• There is no job security, since it is a temporary arrangement with the driver and, in some cases, the owner.

• There is competition for this job, particularly in the city. In such situations, a personal contact will help in finding a place to work.

5.7.2   Legal aspects of the job

• The job is offered only on the basis of a verbal agreement and no documents are exchanged between the owner and a driver and/or conductor.

• The conductors are aware of the need for obtaining a license for conductors. However, since there is no compulsion to do so, they have not bothered to obtain a license.

• The conductors also know about the existence of the Passenger Transport Authority of the Western Provincial Council. It is the main institution responsible for regulating the private bus services.

- They know about passenger loading limits, speed limits within the city and other general traffic rules and regulations. However, they said they are compelled to ignore these regulations due to the competitiveness between bus services and the need to earn a target amount per day to pay back the rental charge to the bus owner.

- The conductors say that due to the increase in the number of route permits issued on Colombo city routes, the buses get limited turns per day. Therefore, they have to earn the maximum possible income per turn to meet their daily target. This has compelled them to take too many passengers on board at every chance they get.

- The Provincial Road Passenger Transport Authority issues a log chart on which the timekeeper at the point of origin and destination enters the time and puts his signature.

- The Authority has also instructed the conductors to issue bus tickets to each and every passenger. However, it is not possible to issue tickets in practice due to heavily crowded conditions. The other issue is that passengers do not ask for tickets. Therefore, some conductors said they did not issue tickets.

5.7.3 Difficulties faced in performing their job

- The unregulated system of private bus operation has been the root cause of many difficulties they face (i.e. lack of a timetable, over supply of buses on the same routes etc.).

- Lack of designated bus stops. This encourages passengers to wait at every street corner trying to get onto buses.

- Managing passengers, particularly at peak hours, is a difficult job. When the bus gets loaded with passengers, issuing tickets becomes a real problem. Many passengers try to avoid paying their fare during peak hours.

- The majority of passengers prefer to stay close to the doors. Therefore, conductors are compelled to shout at them to move away from the doors.

- The conductors have to work long hours (i.e. 12 to 15 hours per day), which is tiring. If they do not work hard for long hours, they will not be able to meet their income targets.

- They do not have an assurance of job security. Therefore, self-respect and self-discipline are not matters that worry them.

- Nor do the passengers respect the conductors, although they are performing an important job, taking people to their required destinations.

- The traffic police often try to find fault with the bus conductors and drivers, even if they do not commit a mistake.

- The conductors have not been provided with any training for their job. Gaining experience has been a hard and difficult exercise for them.

- Many passengers do not think about the passengers' responsibilities when they get onto a bus, rather they expect only that the conductors' behaviour be favourable to them.

- 'We are not satisfied with this job at all. Because, we have to always work under severe tension and heavy pressure from passengers and traffic police,' said some conductors.

- Increasing traffic congestion in the city, as well as the roadside parking of motor vehicles, makes it difficult for buses to operate in the way that passengers wish them to.

- 'We have to assist the driver, too, in addition to managing the passengers. Therefore our job is really a difficult one.'

5.7.4 The positive aspects of the conductors' job

- 'We did not have to go through all those government rules and regulations to find this job. It was an easy job for people who do not have many qualifications like us.'

- 'We can gradually learn driving, too, while working as conductors.'

- 'If we work hard there is always a possibility of earning about 500 to 600 Rupees per day after spending for our meals and paying back the day's rental for the bus.'

- 'When we have about 4 to 5 years of experience we can always find a job in the passenger bus service.'

- 'On certain days of the week we could well exceed our daily target and make additional savings for drivers and ourselves.'

- 'Because we handle money every day, we do not think that any other job might make us happy.'

5.7.5 Suggestions to improve the job of conductors and the bus service

- 'The government must take steps to recognize our job and take steps to make it a permanent job.'

- 'Regular training / awareness programmes should be conducted to educate the conductors and drivers on traffic rules, regulations and ways to improve their performances.'

- 'Awareness programmes should also be conducted to make passengers aware as to how they should behave in a public bus. Their responsibilities and rights must be known to them.'

- 'The government must take initiatives to organize the private bus sector into companies so that the workers would be able to get better recognition and job security.

5.8 Perspectives of private bus drivers on their services

- There is no job security for the private bus drivers.

- The owners change the drivers and conductors regularly.

- Private bus drivers and conductors are not regular employees (mainly in Colombo) and they take the buses on a daily hire basis. Hence, they have to earn the daily hiring charge for the owner as well as an income for the driver and conductor. This situation compels them to earn more money, even violating traffic regulations and taking too many passengers.

- There is no training given to private bus drivers. They have to learn rules and regulations through practice.

- They feel that their job is not recognized by passengers or the general public.

- The transport ministry and traffic control authorities never consult drivers and conductors when introducing traffic rules and regulations.

- Since they have to work to achieve a daily financial target, drivers have to work for more than 12 hours a day.

- There is no strong relationship between the owner, driver and conductor of the buses. Therefore, the maintenance of the vehicle (particularly cleaning the inside) and aspects of reckless driving become normal issues.

- Private bus drivers violate traffic regulations because they have experience that when they break traffic rules for example ten times, they get caught only once or twice by the traffic police. The benefit they acquire through the breaking of traffic regulations is much more than the fine they have to pay when caught by the traffic police.

- In most of the private buses in the city, drivers and conductors are just casual operators of the services. Hence, they have no real obligation to the bus owners or passengers (some drivers come to the city from the countryside to work for five days and then go back home during the weekend; when they come back again they do not get the same bus to work).

5.9   Perspectives of private bus owners

Five bus owners were interviewed who operate their buses within Colombo city and suburbs. Their views on private bus services, operational difficulties, legal aspects and suggestions are described below.

5.9.1   Entering into running a private bus service

- Three of the bus owners said they were attracted by the incentives offered by the government during 1980s to start a private bus service. Investors were particularly attracted to the minimum legal and procedural requirements during the initial stages. The other two interviewees said that they had seen the attractive return enjoyed after this investment by some of their friends. Therefore, they also decided to invest in the purchase of a single bus.

- They all utilized part of their own savings and the leasing arrangements to purchase the buses.

- Initially, three of the owners operated the buses by themselves with conductors. However, later they all decided to employ a driver because they realized that driving a bus on the busy streets of Colombo and its suburbs is an extremely difficult job. On the other hand, the owners have to work for long hours to earn a sufficient income to pay back the loan instalments and to pay the maintenance costs of the bus.

5.9.2   Legal aspects of the bus operation

- The owners were all aware of the regulations imposed by the Road Passenger Transport Authority of the Western Provincial Council (i.e. the issue of route permits, sub route permits, surcharges for any delay in renewing passenger service permits, permit labels, special hire permits etc.)

- They also attended one or two workshops conducted by the Passenger Transport Authority a few years ago.

- The owners were also aware of the government traffic rules and regulations enforced by the city traffic police.

5.9.3 Difficulties encountered by private bus owners

- One of the main difficulties of the owners was earning a sufficient monthly income to cover all the running expenses and to pay the lease instalments to the finance companies.

- During the first two- to three-year period they were able to make regular monthly payments to the crew and operate at a reasonable profit. Subsequently, when repairs became more frequent, it was difficult to operate at a reasonable profit.

- Currently, three out of the five owners rent out their buses on a daily basis to the drivers known to them. The drivers return the bus along with the agreed daily rent to the owner. They said this was a convenient arrangement for them. However, it is always a high-risk option as the drivers who rent the buses operate with little care and in an undisciplined manner.

- The operating of buses on congested city routes has become a problem due to loss of fuel as well as the limited number of turns that the buses can take along a route because of the many competing buses.

- The government is not prepared to offer incentives to the private bus owners in terms of fuel quotas or spare parts without levying taxes etc.

- Most of the city bus routes are already crowded with an over supply of passenger buses. However, the authorities do not properly understand this situation.

5.9.4 Suggestions to improve private bus services

- The government must re-allocate the number of buses on city routes in consultation with the bus owners and users.

- The government must also regulate the traffic flow in the city by allowing specific lanes for passenger buses.

- Provision of concessions to private bus owners, particularly on fuel prices, or allowing them to increase bus fares must be granted.

- The necessary road infrastructure must be improved i.e. traffic lights, wide pavements for pedestrians, undisturbed streets by way of providing off street parking for motor vehicles etc.

Section 6

Para-transport providers

6.1   Perspectives of three-wheeler operators on their service

- There is no proper place on the street to park three-wheelers.

- There was a three-wheeler drivers' association in Colombo, but it was not functioning at the time of the interviews due to fragmentation of its membership.

- It is dangerous to operate three-wheelers at night due to thieves and the hijacking of three-wheelers.

- There are no training and awareness programmes on traffic rules and regulations for three-wheeler drivers.

- There is no social recognition for three-wheeler drivers due to some drivers' involvement in illegal activities.

- Some passengers pressurize three-wheeler drivers to reach a destination quickly, which compels them to take risks.

- Due to the language barrier, most of three-wheeler drivers are not able to provide transport facilities to the foreigners who visit Colombo.

- Sometimes policemen exploit three-wheeler drivers by using them free of charge.

6.2   Perspectives of school van drivers on their job

- There are no proper parking spaces for school vans. The van drivers have to find their own parking spaces. There are no toilet facilities in the city for these people.

- There is no government involvement in the management of school vans.

- Although they carry school children, there is no priority for these vehicles on the streets.

- There are no government organizations to discuss and report on the problems of school van operators.

- The operation of school vans is not recognized by the government as a useful service, although they feel they are performing a responsible duty.

Section 7

Issues raised by the participants at focus group meetings

Two focus group meetings were held in Poorwarama and Badowita case study settlements. Those invited included some of the people who were interviewed before as well as others who were not interviewed as part of the research in order to discuss issues relating to public transport facilities.

- In Poorwarama, 41 persons participated while in Badowita settlement 33 persons attended the focus group meeting.

- The group discussions were facilitated by three members of research team of Sevanatha. The focus group meetings were conducted in December 2001 at Poorwarama and in January 2002 in Badowita settlement. The issues raised at the meetings are listed below.

7.1 Perspectives on the existing bus shelters/stops

- Bus shelters are not properly constructed taking into consideration the needs of passengers. The existing bus stops are not properly maintained. The roofs are damaged, therefore they do not provide shelter to passengers.

- There are no seating facilities in the bus shelters. Bus shelters are badly maintained, dirty places.

- During the night the existing bus stops are often occupied by beggars, drug addicts and thieves. They make them dirty and no one is responsible for maintaining the bus stops.

- Lack of proper bus stops is a problem for the elderly, sick people and school children when they need to wait for long hours to catch a bus.

7.2 Perspectives relating to pedestrian travel

- We have to walk about 20 to 30 minutes to reach the main road. The access road is a gravel road, which is difficult to use on rainy days due to water logging.

- In the evenings, too, young girls and women find it unsafe to walk along these roads because of thieves and other people who harass women.

- Often the pavements are very narrow and are blocked by vendors and motorists. Therefore, we have to get onto the road and walk alongside the pavement, which is risky.

- Most of our roads are also narrow and difficult to accommodate the increasing volume of motor vehicles.

- There are no adequate pavements for pedestrians or separate tracks for cyclists. We would prefer to use pedal cycles, but the road is too congested with motor vehicles.

- Women are harassed by three-wheeler drivers and some people who use the street.

7.3 People's perspectives on regulations relating to passenger transport

- Passengers have no idea about where to make a complaint when bus drivers and conductors do something wrong. Passengers know only about complaining to the police. However, they believe that it will take a long time for the police to take any action or sometimes their complaint will go unheard by the police.

- Since passengers are not taking action against any wrong doing by drivers and conductors, bus crews tend to break traffic rules and regulations and do not pay much attention to the passengers.

- People have no idea about any passenger association or any other civil organization where they can discuss their problems and make suggestions for improving passenger transport services.

7.4 Perspectives about the behaviour of bus conductors and drivers

- Normally, private bus conductors never use a polite language. They always see passengers as problem creators.

- It is a usual thing to observe that conductors of private buses keep on shouting at passengers to move forward or move backward, while moving themselves through passengers inside the bus.

- The conductors often delay returning the change to passengers purposefully so as to cheat them.

- Private bus conductors do not issue tickets to passengers. Passengers also get used to that system and do not bother to ask for a ticket.

- A majority of private bus drivers drive recklessly as if they are always in a competitive race with other buses on the route.

- The drivers normally do not give sufficient time for passengers to get down from the bus. They are in a hurry to speed and race with other buses. Women, elderly persons and school children suffer the most because of such unacceptable behaviour by bus drivers.

7.5 Difficulties faced by people while travelling by bus

- In most private buses, tickets are not issued to passengers, which becomes a problem as the conductors repeatedly ask for money. Sometimes they do not give passengers their change and they cannot ask for it since they do not have a ticket to show them.

- The handrail is too high to hold for women and children.

- In most of the buses, the bell cannot be seen or the roof bell is not working. Therefore, passengers have to ask someone to help them when they want to get off the bus.

- The steps are fixed too high above ground level; women and children cannot get into or out of the buses quickly.

- The interiors of most of the buses are dirty. The seats are dusty and the floor is covered with rubbish.

- The buses are always overcrowded; children and women are the ones who suffer most in overcrowded buses when they travel standing among other passengers.

- There are no notices inside the buses with useful passenger information.

- Due to the lack of proper goods racks, people suffer when they carry heavy baggage.

7.6   Participants' suggestions for improving passenger services

- The existing buses should be managed properly by ensuring that they run to a time-table.

- Strict regulations must be enforced to ensure that conductors issue bus tickets to passengers.

- There should be limits to how many passengers each bus is allowed to take.

- Overloading should be banned.

- Bells and handrails should be fixed at a convenient height for women and children.

- The bells must be visible to all passengers.

- Those bus owners and bus crews who do not keep their buses cleaned must be fined.

- The bus seats must be fixed with adequate spacing between, and should be of a proper standard.

- The steps should be constructed at a lower level than at present.

- Passenger awareness programmes must be carried out regularly for drivers and conductors to educate them on their rights and responsibilities.

Section 8

Activities of passenger associations

It has been observed that there are no active passenger associations in Sri Lanka. The only passenger movement was formed in the year 1957, soon after the 'Peoplization' of bus transport in Sri Lanka in 1956. The first passenger movement was named the 'All Ceylon Passenger Movement'. Later it was renamed the 'All Ceylon Congress of Passenger Associations'. Presently, this association is known as the Sri Lanka Congress of Passenger Associations.

The Sri Lanka Congress of Passenger Associations was very active during the early 1970s under the able chairmanship of the Ceylon Transport Board (CTB). The Transport Ministry provided the required institutional and infrastructure support for carrying out the activities of the association. The chairman of the CTB allocated one day of the week to meet the officials of the passenger association. Further, he encouraged the officials of the passenger association to visit other regions of Sri Lanka and to form passenger associations since the original association was formed in Colombo. The Ministry of Transport provided free tickets/passes to those officials of the association who wished to visit other parts of Sri Lanka for the above purpose.

Starting from the Colombo Central Passenger Association, about 180 associations were formed throughout the country during the early 1970s. In those days issues relating to CTB passenger transport were discussed with the officials concerned.

Subsequently, with the shift in government policies towards privatization and opening up the economy, the importance given to passengers/users of public transport began to fade. No government support was provided to the passenger associations.

After private buses began to dominate the road passenger transport services in the early 1980s, the difficulties faced by passengers became almost the norm. The Sri Lanka Congress of Passenger Associations became more active as a result. However, it was disappointing to note that the passengers who faced difficulties did not show much interest in joining the association or supporting its activities. Also, the government's support to the association was not very significant.

Thus, as at present, only about 60 passenger associations are in operation in Sri Lanka of which about 21 are located in Western Province.

8.1 Specific activities performed by the Sri Lanka Congress of Passenger Associations

- Publishing newspaper articles on passenger-related issues.

- Organizing public seminars and workshops to discuss the problematic aspects of passenger transport in Sri Lanka.

- Representing the passengers' views at the Ministry forums.

- Participating in advisory committee meetings and forums.

- Receiving complaints and requests from passenger from all parts of the country and submitting them to the relevant authorities.

8.2 The limitations faced by the Congress of Passenger Associations

- There is no government support as there was in the past (particularly during the 1970s) to further the activities of the passenger associations.

- The Association has no funds or manpower resources to organize passengers throughout the country.

- The passengers who face difficulties in using public bus transport do not show any interest in initiating local actions; instead they have become passive users.

- Passengers have no faith in the regulatory system of public transport, hence they tend to find different alternatives, such as organizing their own transport, or suffer the problems of the system in silence.

Section 9

Private bus owners association of Sri Lanka

Views expressed by the president of the Association.

9.1   How was the Association formed?

The organization was formed in March 2001. The private bus companies operating in different parts of Sri Lanka got together and formed it. At the initial stage the private bus companies operating in Nugegoda, Negambo, Kaduwela, Kurunagala participated in forming the association. Later many other companies also joined. They included private bus companies from Galle, Kandy, Kandy North, Mahiyanganaya, Matara, Kundasale, Polonnaruwa, Anuradhapura, Awissawella, Bulathsinhala, Kegalle, Maharagama and Kottawa.

The bus owners are connected to the Association only through the private bus companies that have formed in different areas. Each bus company has to pay 100 Rupees to the Association to become a member.

9.2   The meetings of the Association.

Monthly meetings are conducted involving official representatives (President, Secretary, Treasure) of the member companies. The problems faced by bus owners and companies are discussed at the meetings and solutions to those problems are agreed on. The Association is registered under the Western Province Road Passenger Transport Authority. It has the powers to discuss issues with the Ministry and government institutions concerned. The association has estimated that about 70 per cent of the passengers of Sri Lanka rely on private bus transport. However, the majority of passengers have negative attitudes towards the quality of private bus transport. Therefore it is very important to carry out programs to change the attitudes of general public towards private transport services.

9.3   The difficulties faced by the members of the Private Bus Association

- One of the key difficulties of owners is the payment of heavy instalments to finance companies. Most of the private bus owners purchased buses on finance company guarantees. They have to pay large sums of money (about 30,000 to 40,000 Rupees per month) to finance companies. Therefore, the bus owners keep trying to meet maximum daily income targets. This leads to many complaints by the passengers.

- Secondly, the poor management of private sector buses by the government creates problems for earning the targeted amounts. The lack of a specific timetable and control of journeys have lead to losses in income as well as creating conflicts among the bus drivers.

- The government and the provincial councils have not paid adequate attention to managing the inter-provincial transport systems so as to provide better services to passengers.

- A lack of reliable, trained drivers and committed conductors has been another severe problem when running private buses. Most bus operators are casual workers; they have no serious attachment to their jobs because of the casual nature of their work. Drivers and conductors pay attention only to earning their day targets and this leads to the dissatisfaction of passengers.

- The government's rules for issuing conductor licenses have created problems due to proof of residency within the locality. Conductors who come from outside Colombo can't get a license due to their lack of occupancy in the area they work. These regulations should therefore be changed.

- There are no adequate spaces on most of the city roads to park the buses while they are waiting for their turn to travel a route. Most of the roadside spaces are blocked by three-wheelers and other motor vehicles. Therefore the lack of parking spaces has become a serious problem for private bus owners in the city.

- There are no facilities, such as toilets, water and waiting rooms etc. for private bus drivers at the city transport terminals.

9.4 Suggestions for improving the quality of private bus services

- The government must recognize the importance of the private bus service and provide proper legal support to operate it with dignity.

- Facilities must be provided for parking, along with other facilities for drivers at large and small terminals.

- Programmes should be introduced so that the jobs of private bus drivers and conductors become recognized as professional employment.

- Financial support must be provided to private bus owners to purchase new buses and to maintain the condition of their existing buses.

- There must be some control over the overall traffic in the city and space must be provided for passenger transport buses.

Section 10

Affordability of public transport service

It is significant to note that the majority of interviewees have indicated that the existing bus fares are not too high for them to afford. At present the starting bus fare is Rs. 3 (three Rupees), which is increasing by 50 cents per section. On average, the ordinary bus fare in Sri Lanka is around 50 cents per km. Semi luxury buses charge about 1½ times the normal rate, while luxury buses charge twice the normal bus fare. The bus fare structure is controlled and decided by the Ministry of Transport on recommendations by the National Transport Commission and other related institutions; hence the bus owners and operators cannot decide on the bus fares. This was an important aspect of regularization of one aspect of public transport.

It is accepted that the existing bus fares are generally affordable for every section of society in Sri Lanka. This may be the reason that none of the interviewees pointed out the bus fares as an issue of concern. Rather, all of them commented on the poor quality of the buses and bus services.

In order to understand the relative importance of transport expenditure among other expenditures, these have been examined using the data available on consumer finances and a socio-economic survey of Sri Lanka in 1996/97. It was found that the overall average percentage on transport expenditure was about 12.4 per cent for all sectors (rural, urban and plantation sectors) in the country.

Table 10.1. Comparison of monthly income and monthly transport expenses of 30 households of case study settlements

Income category (Rupees per month)	Monthly transport expenditures	%
Up to 5,000	444	8.9
5,001 – 8,000	573	8.8
8,001 – 11,000*	686	8.1
Over 11,000*	300	2.7

*The households whose incomes were above Rs.8001 were those who run small boutiques and those who have their family members working abroad. The boutique owners said they do not need to travel outside the settlement since the delivery vans and mobile traders brings items to the boutique. Hence, their transport expenses were said to be low. They do not own motor vehicles either.

Table 10.2. Percentage of expenditure for one month on non-durable items by income groups

Item	0 – 300	301 – 600	601 – 1,200	1,201 – 1,800	1,801 – 2,400	2,401 – 3,000	3,001 – 4,500	4,501 – 6,000	6,001 – 7,500	7,501 – 9,000	9,001 – 12,000	12,001 – 15,000	15,001 – 30,000	Over 30,000	Overall Average
Housing	6.0	3.2	12.6	19.3	16.6	16.9	18.1	19.8	23.4	26.1	25.1	26.7	28.7	30.0	25.2
Clothing	12.3	10.8	19.9	14.7	17.2	17.7	18.7	16.1	15.5	16.6	16.1	13.4	13.7	10.0	14.7
Fuel & Light	5.8	3.7	12.0	17.3	15.3	15.4	14.4	12.5	11.3	10.8	8.6	8.0	6.5	4.3	9.0
Transport	11.2	3.5	8.5	8.4	10.5	8.2	8.0	9.6	8.8	11.1	11.9	11.0	15.6	17.6	12.4
Education	-	0.6	2.6	4.1	4.5	3.7	5.0	5.7	5.6	5.3	5.5	5.3	5.7	5.0	5.4
Recreation	6.7	1.0	3.1	2.3	2.3	2.5	2.9	3.4	3.4	3.4	3.9	3.6	3.2	3.3	3.3
Social Expenses	4.0	0.4	2.4	5.9	7.9	7.2	9.1	10.7	11.8	8.1	10.5	13.1	8.4	11.9	10.2
Personal Expenses	11.9	42.9	5.0	6.9	6.9	8.0	7.5	7.3	6.6	6.4	5.5	5.3	4.5	3.1	5.5
Servants / Drivers	-	-	2.1	0.5	0.1	0.1	0.0	0.1	0.2	0.2	0.5	0.6	1.6	6.3	1.4
Medical	0.4	4.4	6.2	8.1	6.4	6.6	5.8	6.1	6.1	4.9	5.6	5.5	6.2	3.5	5.5
Other Non-Durable	41.7	29.4	25.6	12.4	12.2	13.6	10.6	8.8	7.3	7.0	6.9	7.4	5.9	4.9	7.3
Total	100.0	100.0	100.0	100.0	100.0	100.0	100.0	100.0	100.0	100.0	100.0	100.0	100.0	100.0	100.0

An analysis of randomly selected 30 households from all the six case study settlements illustrated that the percentage share of transport expenses as against their monthly income was in the range of 2.7 per cent to 8.9 per cent

The above information revealed that the affordability of public transport has not been a major problem for the low-income communities in Colombo. However, they are much more concerned with the quality of bus services and operational problems. The information gathered through the present survey on bus fares spent by households corresponds with the findings of the other reports, such as the Annual Report of Central Bank, which say the public bus fares in Sri Lanka are affordable by even low-income people, since the bus fares are relatively low compared to most other services.

Section 11

Major issues identified through the research project

Through interviews of key informants and resource persons, as well as a review of the available literature, a multitude of issues have been identified relating to public transport services. Different categories of people (i.e. the users (passengers), the providers, the service crews and regulatory personnel) have been interviewed in order to obtain their perspectives on the current situation and what they would like to see and experience in the future. All these issues are listed in the previous section of this report. Hence, this chapter is devoted to the most common issues raised by the interviewees. This is because it is believed that those issues that are raised by many people on several occasions are the most serious problems or situations as far as those particular groups are concerned. In this context, the issues raised by the interviewees are listed under the following key groups.

i)   Users (passengers) of public transport

ii)   Providers of public transport

iii) Service crews

iv)   Regulators of public transport

11.1 Major issues relating to users (passengers) of public transport

i)   Lack of properly planned and maintained bus stops / bus shelters on the streets. This major issue has contributed to the creation of several sub-issues which, in turn, affect the quality of passenger transport and cause inconvenience to passengers, accidents, traffic congestion and so on.

ii)   Lack of properly designed pavements for pedestrian travel. The existing pavements are too narrow, poorly constructed and not maintained, and are blocked by pavement hawkers and motorists. Hence, children, women, disabled people and other ordinary pedestrians must risk walking along existing pavements. Lack of proper pavements discourages even those who wish to walk, mainly due to the inconvenience and risk of having an accident.

iii) Poorly planned pedestrian crossings on busy streets are of little help to pedestrians. Due to poor understanding of pedestrians' rights and the responsibilities of motorists, the crossings do not provide their intended benefits.

iv) Lack of passenger information at bus stops, on street crossings and other public meeting points on passenger safety and available transport services, were highlighted by all categories of passengers interviewed.

v) Passengers have no knowledge of to whom they should complain when they face problems while travelling on buses.

vi) Lack of safety for pedestrians (especially for women and girls) because of potential accidents, theft and harassment by thugs, is a major concern by almost all the interviewees.

vii) Competition among bus drivers leads to reckless driving, causing road accidents and risking the lives of passengers who use private buses.

viii) The interior conditions of the buses and the facilities available were described as being totally inadequate and inappropriate for passengers. People feel that the interior design of buses does not consider the needs of passengers of different age groups and different abilities. Hence a majority of passengers were unhappy about the facilities available inside the buses.

ix) The passengers also identified the undisciplined behaviour of private bus conductors, particularly their harassment of women and children, cheating of passengers' money and shouting at passengers for no reason. All such problems seem to be related to a lack of proper training and the lack of respect for the job.

x) The reckless and undisciplined driving of private bus drivers was a major concern for the majority of interviewees. They put it down to poor law enforcement on the part of government, as well as poor training of the drivers of private buses by the authorities concerned.

xi) Lack of limits for the number of passengers that buses are allowed to take, particularly in private buses, was a growing concern raised by many passengers. Women, school children and disabled people were the worst affected passengers as a result of this uncontrolled loading.

xii) Poor street planning, poor control of motor traffic, lack of parking and air pollution created by motor traffic seem to have severely discouraged the use of more environmental friendly and affordable transport modes, such as walking and cycling.

xiii) A large majority of passengers pointed out the lack of knowledge on the part of the general public as to their rights and responsibilities as passengers and pedestrians. This has also been contributed to by inactivity of the government.

xiv) None of the interviewees were worried about bus fares since they consider them to be affordable. Rather, they were worried about the quality of the buses as well as operational problems, particularly those relating to the bus crews.

11.2 Major issues raised by the providers of public transport (owners and owners' associations)

i) A majority of bus owners are engaged in providing bus services as operators of individually-owned buses. Their motivation has always been to earn an income that makes a profit on their investment. Due to competition with the unlimited number of private buses on the roads and high running costs, their profits margin have been reduced. Therefore, operating to a strict timetable, keeping the bus crews on a permanent basis and providing a decent service to passengers have become matters of less concern to them.

ii) Lack of government subsidies and / or incentives to private bus owners seems to have prevented them from providing an efficient, reliable transport service to passengers.

iii) Lack of proper guidance, rules and regulations at the initial stages of operating their bus service led private bus owners to begin their business without proper knowledge. Reversing that situation with the introduction of controls has become a difficult task for the government.

iv) Lack of properly planned streets, bus stops, parking and terminal facilities for the operation of passenger bus services in the city has lead to severe traffic congestion, road accidents, wasted time for passengers, loss of income for bus owners and heavy operational costs.

v) Due to the poor management of passenger transport services by the government, most of the city routes have become too congested with an over supply of passenger transport vehicles. This, in turn, leads to undisciplined driving, as well as difficulty in controlling the city traffic.

vi) The three-wheeler operators have also become a problem as far as the city traffic is concerned. Lack of designated parking spaces, lack of fares regulation and undisciplined driving by the three-wheeler drivers contribute to road accidents and traffic congestion in the city.

vii) Due to the poor school bus services provided by the government, private individuals have started operating school van services. Lack of proper planning and infrastructure for this category of vehicles has further aggravated already congested city traffic, as well as increased accidents. It was estimated by the interviewees that there were about seven thousand school vans that enter the city of Colombo daily. Imagine the situation created in the city with no proper parking and no designated lanes for such a large number of vehicles.

11.3 Major issues raised by the crew of public transport services (mainly bus drivers and conductors)

i) The private bus conductors and drivers have identified their jobs as being only temporary. There is no sense of permanency to these occupations and therefore there is no professional value or respect attachment to them.

ii) A majority of drivers and conductors hire out a bus on a daily basis and operate it to earn an income to cover that rent plus a profit. This situation has lead to undisciplined driving and the breaking of traffic rules and regulations, as well as to a lack of respect or sympathy towards passengers.

iii) Poor social recognition of bus crews and ineffective law enforcement, in turn, compel them to behave in an undisciplined manner.

iv) Private bus owners employ a limited number of bus crew members and hence the drivers and conductors have to work long hours (12 to 15 hours) of the day (i.e. starting from 4.30 or 5.00 a.m. and working until 7.30 or 8.00 p.m.) for about five or six days per week. Under such a hard working arrangement, the bus crews seem to have become impatient, undisciplined and irresponsible.

v)   Lack of proper work related training or monitoring has lead to an unsatisfactory performance by the bus crews, which in turn is reflected in their poor relationship with customers as well as their irresponsible behaviour.

11.4   Major issues raised by regulatory bodies and personnel

i.   There are a number of regulatory agencies in Sri Lanka whose job it is to guide and regulate public transport services. However, due to a lack of proper co-ordination at the national as well as the city level, these agencies are not able to properly address the problems relating to public transport or provide a quality service to the public.

ii.   The privatization of public transport came as a political decision around the 1980s, one that was seemingly implemented with no consideration given to the potential problems that it might create.

iii. The intended outcome of competition between the government owned bus service and the private bus service never became a reality. This was due to the difficulties of running these two services with the similar objective of providing better services to passengers, and because the private bus service put greater emphasis on making a profit rather than providing a service. Therefore, the private bus service completed with government buses on the same route, getting more passengers and eventually wiping out the government buses.

iv.   Organizing the individually-operated private bus service into companies in order to achieve smooth operation has become very difficult.

v.   There is a lack of strong political commitment to regularize the operation of private buses due to pressure from businessmen and influential people who are engaged in the private bus operation.

vi.   The above-mentioned unregulated system of private bus services has compelled the government owned buses to operate on non-profitable routes while most profitable routes are being taken by the private bus operators. This situation eventually resulted in the non-operation of buses on non-economical routes, preventing some passengers from using any form of public transport service.

vii. The traffic police and Colombo Municipal Council are engaged in controlling traffic conditions in the city of Colombo. However, due to the increasing inflow of motor vehicles (according to the city traffic police, over 300,000 vehicles enter the city daily), with no adequate road / traffic infrastructure to cater to this demand, there has been an increase in road accidents and air pollution, a loss of working hours and, above all, citizens have been caused severe inconvenience.

viii. The regulatory agency personnel emphasized the lack of co-operation of the general public who use the city streets and public transport, as well as the unco-operative attitudes of motorists in observing existing traffic rules and regulations. Civil society groups do not provide any suggestions to overcome the current crises of public transport. Therefore, it has become difficult for the regulatory agencies to solve the problems relating to passenger transport services in Colombo alone.

ix.   With respect to partnerships among the transport providers, it has been observed that there are no significant partnership arrangements in operation. The intended partnership between the CTB and private bus operation has proved to be unrealistic. The other para-transport modes (school vans, three-wheelers, office staff transport vans etc.) are also operated mostly on an individual basis with no proper partnership arrangements. Therefore, the issue of partnership arrangements among different modes of transport operators, as well as of the users and regulators, must be considered seriously in the future.

Section 12

Recommendations

12.1 Recommendations made by the interviewees on major issues

The respondents not only raised issues relating to various aspects of public transport services, but also made recommendations as to how these issues may be tackled. With the purpose of differentiating the emphasis made by the key actors, the recommendations are presented under the following categories:.

i)   Users (passengers) of public transport

ii)   Providers of public transport

iii)   Service crews

iv)   Regulators of public transport

i)   Recommendations made by users (passengers) of public transport

* The bus stops must be properly planned and bus shelters with seating facilities should be constructed. The shelters must be properly maintained and provided with passenger information.

* The city streets must be constructed with wider pavements, free of obstructions, and must be devoted to the convenient use of passengers of all ages. Particular emphasis must be paid to the needs of the disabled, elderly people, women and children.

* Pedestrian crossings must be planned at convenient places. Pedestrian crossings at busy junctions must be provided with coloured lights in order to ensure the safety of pedestrians. The crossings must be used to display passenger-related information.

* Continuous awareness programmes must be carried out using mass media and other appropriate communication methods to educate passengers on traffic rules and regulations and the responsibilities of passengers and motorists, as well as the places and persons to whom complaints and requests can be made.

* Passengers have especially recommended that reckless drivers of public bus services, and other motorists who purposefully violate traffic rules and regulations, must be fined. If the current laws are not adequate the authorities must introduce new laws to control the undisciplined behaviour of motorists.

- Programmes must be implemented to develop a good relationship between the conductors, drivers and the passengers of public bus transport. Particular attention should be paid to changing the attitudes of private bus conductors towards the passengers.

- The authorities must take action to implement passenger load limits on private buses, since the passengers who pay their fares must have the right to travel conveniently on the buses.

- Serious attention must be paid to redesigning the interior facilities of buses, such as the seats, the spaces between seats, the handrails, the bells and the steps. This is because the present designs do not seem to have considered the needs of elderly people, women, children or even disabled people. Therefore, a majority of passengers suffer while travelling on buses.

- The interviewees emphasized the fact that our cities are poorly planned. They would prefer streets with wide pavements and less congestion, with appropriate parking spaces for vehicles. (Some of the interviewees mentioned that they would like to see a development of our streets similar to those shown on television in developed countries.)

ii)   Recommendations made by providers of public transport

- The government must intervene in co-ordinating private bus operations in order to provide efficient services to the public, while at the same time providing opportunities for the owners to earn a sufficient income.

- Public transport-related infrastructure facilities must be developed particularly parking spaces for passenger buses so that private bus services can operate smoothly.

- The route allocation system must be streamlined in order to prevent over supply of buses on some routes, while others do not get sufficient buses.

- Concessionary loan repayment schemes and / or fuel subsidies must be provided to private bus operators in order to make up for increasing running costs.

- The private bus transport services must be properly organized and must be recognized as important services since they takes over 60 per cent of road passengers in Sri Lanka at present.

iii)   Recommendations made by service crew (conductors and drivers)

- The employment status of private bus conductors and drivers must be upgraded using proper training, recognition and a system of assuring permanency of employment.

- The working conditions of the private bus crews must be changed so as to address the stress of long working hours and their dissatisfaction with their employment.

- There is also a need for awareness-raising among the passengers, particularly with respect to their use of the streets, pedestrian crossings and helping bus conductors in performing their duties.

iv)   Recommendations made by regulators of public transport

- Regulators of public transport services recognize the complex nature of the operation of public transport services in Sri Lanka. Improving co-ordination of the activities of various agencies involved in the sector was emphasized.

- Provision of the infrastructure facilities that are required for adequate public transport services should be given high priority.

- Rules and regulations to ensure proper management of city traffic, with strict enforcement of traffic regulations, must be introduced.

- The regulators recognized the importance of creating public awareness, particularly that of passengers (including school children), on traffic rules and regulations so as to improve the road discipline of passengers and motorists.

12.2 Framework for policy recommendations

Based on the perspectives of key actors on the current status of public transport, and the issues identified through the research, it was considered appropriate to develop a framework for policy recommendations. These recommendations eventually could lead to strategic actions to improve access to and the quality of public transport. The proposed policy framework does not attempt to address the complex issues of transport sector policies in a holistic sense. However, in keeping with the scope of the current research project it attempts to emphasize previously neglected aspects of user perspectives in the formation of a holistic transport policy. This is because it was revealed to be important to consider the views of the users, who are the real target group of public transport. In this context, the proposed policy framework can be developed considering the following aspects.

Key principles of the policy frame work:

- Issue-based

- Target-oriented

- Consultative process

- Partnership actions

- Participatory monitoring

Issue-based
The proposed policy framework should be based on the key issues raised by the users as well as those raised by the other actors who are engaged in public transport services. This will prevent the policymakers from resorting to identification of perceived issues through a non-consultative process of using hard data relating to the key actors.

Target-oriented
It was disappointing to note that most of the conventional policy documents only spell out policy issues with no reference to specific targets to be achieved. Hence, the proposed policy framework must emphasize specific target issues, time bond actions and the results to be achieved in transport services.

Consultative process
The target population should be consulted prior to the identification of issues and the necessary actions that must be taken. Consultation should be developed as a process. The users, the providers and the public transport regulators must be given opportunities to continue the process of consultation, both individually and among groups. The government must genuinely promote the process of consultation among the key actors by

way of institutionalization of the consultation process as part of its policy formulation so that real issues can be identified and practical solutions can be formulated.

Partnership actions

At present there is no partnership arrangement in operation in the transport sector. As a result appropriate legal and institutional actions must be incorporated into the transport sector in order to promote workable partnerships between different actors/partners engaged in provision of public transport services.

Participatory monitoring

Impacts of policies should be monitored through a participatory monitoring process. This would allow actors at different levels to provide live examples of implementation successes and failures. Forums of specific groups of actors can be used as an effective and efficient approach to participatory monitoring of policy implementation.

The policymakers at the national and the provincial levels can use the above framework in order to create a sustainable interaction between the government authorities and different categories of actors, including the users of public transport services who will ultimately experience policy directives and actions in real life.

Research Advisory Committee (RAC)

	Name and address	Focus of action/ representation	Contact details
1	Mr. John Diandas, Transport Consultant 35, Galle Face Court 02, Colombo 03	Transport expert / researcher	324313(o) 324313 (f) 433512 (r)
2	Mr. Gunatilake Banda, Deputy Director, Transport Planning, Urban Development Authority, Sethsiripaya Battaramulla	Policy and planning	888561(o) 610132 (r) 872260 (f)
3	Dr. D.S. Jayaweera, Deputy Director (Planning), Ministry of Transport	Policy, planning & implementation	669305 (o)/(f)
4	Dr. Amal Kumarage, Senior Lecturer, Dept of Civil Engineering, University of Moratuwa, Katubedda.	Transport expert, policy, planning and research	650567, 650568 (o) 646702 (r)
5	Mr. U.A. Leelananda, Superintending Engineer (Studies), Colombo Municipal Council (CMC), Town Hall.	Policy, planning and infrastructure	686605 691191 ext. 267
6	Mr. Ajith Ranjith, Assist. Operation Manager, Road Passenger Transport Authority – Western Province, No. 59, Robert Gunawardana Mawatha, Battaramulla	Regulation	871354 (o) 871353 (f)
7	Mr. H.A. Karunasena, Secretary, *Marga Mituro* (Friends on Roads), C/o JBIC, No. 42, Nawam Mawatha, Colombo 02	Passengers and pedestrians	300470-2
8	Mr. D.M.A.S.W. Munasinghe, Transportation Superintendent (Planning), Sri Lanka Railways, Railway Head Quarters, Colombo 10	Railway service providers	435845 (o/f) rlypln@visual.lk
9	Mrs Mandrie J. Sahabandu, No. 19, Charlemont Road, Colombo 06 (former Director General of the National Transport Commission)	Transport expert/ researcher	582741 (r)
10	Mr. Kumudu Kusum Kumara Senior Lecturer, Department of Sociology, Faculty of Arts, University of Colombo, Colombo	Sociologist	500452 (o) 522045 (r)
11	Mr. Sunil Colambage, Committee member, All Ceylon Private Bus Owners' Association (Home Address: 75 A, Dutugemunu Street, Kalubowila, Dehiwala)	Service providers	956427 (r)
12	Mr. K. A. Jayaratne, Chairman, Sevanatha Urban Resource Centre, 14, School Lane, Nawala, Rajagiriya	Urban Planning / management	878893 (o)

(o) – office, (r) – residence, (f) – fax

**Research team of Sevanatha,
the urban resource centre who engaged in the project**

Core research team

- K.A. Jayaratne — Overall guidance
- H.M.U. Chularathna — Research Project Co-ordinator
- D.G.J. Premakumara — Assistant Project Co-ordinator
- K.K.R.P. Kulatilake — Project Co-ordinator
  (from 1st October 2001 to 31st January 2002)

Field research staff

- H.M.D.S.K. Senaviratne — Research Assistant
- I.G.S. Jayasooriya — Research Assistant
- Y.P. Liyanage — Research Assistant

Support staff

- Dilrukshi Silva — Computer Processing of the Report

Overall guidance and supervision

- Dr. M. Sohail Khan — Research Manager,
  Institute of Development Engineering,
  WEDC, Loughborough University, UK

List of references

1. Asian Institute of Transport Development (1996) *Non-Motorised Transport in India—Current Status and Policy Issues*. New Delhi, India.

2. Barter, A.R.P. (2000) *Taking Steps: A Community Action Guide to People-centred, Equitable and Sustainable Urban Transport*. The SUSTRAN Network, Kuala Lampur, Malaysia.

3. CRDS (1994*) Impact of Devolution on the Public Bus Services (CRDS monograph series No. 21).*CRDS: Colombo, Sri Lanka.

4. Dorgi, L. (1996) Bhutan: Economy and Transport System. *Asian Transport Journal*, Asian Institute of Transport Development: New Delhi, India, pp. 9–51.

5. Diandas, J. (1988) 'Notes for Benefit Comparison of Government Sector and Private Sector Supplied Bus Services,' in: Friedrich-Ebert-Stiftung *Aspects of Privatization in Sri Lanka*, Colombo, Sri Lanka, pp. 46–62.

6. Fouracre, P.R. *et al.* (1987) *Travel Demand Characteristics in Three Medium Sized Indian Cities*. Transport and Road Research Laboratory: Berkshire, UK.

7. Kumarage, A.S. (1999) *A Policy Proposal for Managing Land Transport in Sri Lanka—A Vision for the Next Millennium: Revised Green Paper for Discussion only.* Chartered Institute of Transport (Sri Lanka): Colombo.

8. *Marga Arakshawa saha Padikayan Muhunapana Getalu Pilibanda Sammanthranaya (Road Safety and Issues faced by Pedestrians) –September 28, 1998.* Management Unit of the Provincial Council, Ministry of Provincial Councils and Provincial Administration.

9. Maunder, D.A.C. (1990) *The Impact of Bus Regulatory Policy in Five African Cities*. Transport and Road Research Laboratory: Berkshire, UK.

10. Ministry of Finance and Planning (1989) *Public Investment Plan 198 –1993*. Ministry of Finance and Planning, Colombo, Sri Lanka.

11. National Planning Division (1984) *Public Investment 1984–1988*. Ministry of Finance and Planning: Colombo, Sri Lanka.

12. National Transport Commission (1997) *Project for Specialized Training for Crews and Road Staff in Road Passenger Transport: Short Term Plan Training for Existing Crews*, (unpublished report). Colombo, Sri Lanka.

13. Org-Marg Smart *et al.* (2001) *Market Research Study on Railway Passenger Service—Qualitative Research.*

14. Padam, S. (1996) "Transport and Regulatory Practices". *Asian Transport Journal*, pp. 89–97. Asian Institute of Transport Development: New Delhi, India.

15. Raghavan, S.N. (March 1996), "Private Sector in Transport Services and Infrastructure", *Asian Transport Journal*, Asian Institute of Transport Development, New Delhi, pp. 71-89.

16. Ranasinghe P.C.H. (1988) in: Diandas J. (ed.) *Private Bus Transport in Sri Lanka: Its performance, productivity and manpower.* Friedrich-Ebert-Stiftung: Colombo, Sri Lanka.

17. Reddy, Y.V. *et al.* (1996) "Regulatory Policies and Practices: The Case for Reorientation". *Asian Transport Journal*, pp. 49–74. Asian Institute of Transport Development: New Delhi, India.

18. Sohail, M. *et al.* (2001) *Partnerships to Improve Access and Quality of Public Transport for the Urban Poor—Draft Inception Report.* Department for International Development: London, UK.

19. Sohail, M. (ed.) (2000) *Urban Public Transport and Sustainable Livelihoods for the Poor—A Case Study: Karachi, Pakistan.* Water, Engineering and Development Centre: Loughborough University, UK.

20. South Asia 1 Infrastructure Division of the World Bank and the Government of Sri Lanka (1996) *Sri Lanka Transport Sector Strategy Study.* Colombo, Sri Lanka.

21. Stiftung, Friedrich-Ebert (1988) 'Governmentization and Privatization in Transport' in: Friedrich-Ebert-Stiftung *Aspects of Privatization in Sri Lanka*, Colombo, Sri Lanka, pp. 63–84.

22. Stiftung, Friedrich-Ebert (1988) 'The Future of Government-owned Bus Transport in Sri Lanka in: Friedrich-Ebert-Stiftung *Aspects of Privatization in Sri Lanka*, Colombo, Sri Lanka, pp. 85–120.

23. Storm, U.E. (2001) *Establishing Public-Private Partnerships for Railways: Analysis of Public Passenger Transport in the Colombo Suburban Area* (a report submitted to CPCS Transcom Limited and the Asian Development Bank).

24. Townsend, C. (2000) "Implications of Urban Transport Infrastructure Development". *Asia ecoBest,* Vol. 2, No 4, pp. 1–3.

Relevant Acts, Ordinances and Gazettes

1. Ceylon Government Railway Ordinance, 1891

2. Vehicle Ordinance Act No.4 of 1916

3. Motor Car Ordinance No.20 of 1927

4. Motor Car Ordinance No.45 of 1938

5. Omnibus Service Licensing Ordinance No.47 of 1942

6. Motor Traffic Act No.14 of 1951

7. Ceylon Transport Board Act No.48 of 1957

8. Regional Transport Boards Act No.19 of 1978

9. Private Omnibus Service Act No.44 of 1983

10. Peoplized Transport Companies Act No.23 of 1987

11. Motor Traffic Act (Chapter 203) (Incorporating Amendments up to 30 September 1990) 1990

12. National Transport Commission Act No.37 of 1991

13. National Transport Commission (Amendment) Act No.30 of 1996

14. The Gazette of the Democratic Socialist Republic of Sri Lanka No.912/ —Monday, February 26, 1996 – Part IV (A) – Provincial Councils (Regulations under the Western Provincial Road Passenger Carriage Services Statute, No.1 of 1992 and as amended by Statute, No.3 of 1993 and No.7 of 1995

Distribution of low-income families by wards in Colombo Municipal Council

Ward	Total no. of families
Milagiriya	135
Havelock Town	227
Kotahena East	312
Bambalapitiya	360
Cinamon Garden	463
Pamankada-east	468
Wellawatta South	579
Borella-south	620
Tibirigasyaya	709
Aluthkade West	736
Pamankada-west	785
Suduwella	960
Kochchikade South	971
Kollupitiya	998
Kochchikade North	1,003
Maradana	1,019
Kuppiyawatta-east	1,075
Masangas Street	1,121
Kuppiyawatta-west	1,183
Wellawatta North	1,300
Keselwatta	1,304
Aluthkade East	1,436
Lunupokuna	1,521
Kirillapone	1,630
Newbazar	1,650
Maligakanda	1,699
Maligawatta East	1,714
Aluthmawatha	1,738
Modara	1,835
Wekanda	1,952
Slave Island	2,088
Narahenpita	2,166

Distribution of low-income families by wards in Colombo Municipal Council

Ward	Total no. of families
Jinthupitiya	2,231
Maligawatta West	2,272
Dematagoda	2,370
Borella-north	2,433
Wanathamulla	2,476
Hunupitiya	2,538
Kotahena West	2,586
Bluemandel	2,816
Kirula	2,836
Grandpass North	2,998
Mattakkuliya	3,085
Grandpass South	3,214
Panchikawatta	3,310
Mahawatta	6,692
Total	77,614

Distribution of low-income families by wards in Colombo Municipal Council

No. of Families	Ward
Less than 500	Milagiriya
	Havelock Town
	Kotahena East
	Bambalapitiya
	Cinamon Garden
	Pamankada-east
501 – 1,000	Wellawatta South
	Borella-south
	Tibirigasyaya
	Aluthkade West
	Pamankada-west
	Suduwella
	Kochchikade South
	Kollupitiya

Distribution of low-income families by wards in Colombo Municipal Council

No. of Families	Ward
1,001 – 1,500	Kochchikade North
	Maradana
	Kuppiyawatta-east
	Masangas Street
	Kuppiyawatta-west
	Wellawatta North
	Keselwatta
	Aluthkade East
1,501 – 2,000	Lunupokuna
	Kirillapone
	Newbazar
	Maligakanda
	Maligawatta East
	Aluthmawatha
	Modara
	Wekanda
2,001 – 2,500	Slave Island
	Narahenpita
	Jinthupitiya
	Maligawatta West
	Dematagoda
	Borella-north
	Wanathamulla
2,501 – 3,000	Hunupitiya
	Kotahena West
	Bluemandel
	Kirula
	Grandpass North
More than 3,001	Mattakkuliya
	Grandpass South
	Panchikawatta
	Mahawatta